Sawaneh-i Dehli

BIOGRAPHY OF DELHI

OTHER TITLES TRANSLATED BY ATHER FAROUQUI

Munshi Faizuddin	*The Last Gathering: A Vivid Portrait of Life in the Red Fort*

OTHER LOTUS TITLES

Anil Dharker	*Icons: Men & Women Who Shaped Today's India*
Aitzaz Ahsan	*The Indus Saga: The Making of Pakistan*
Ajay Mansingh	*Firaq Gorakhpuri: The Poet of Pain & Ecstasy*
Alam Srinivas	*Women of Vision: Nine Business Leaders in Conversation*
Amarinder Singh	*The Last Sunset: The Rise & Fall of the Lahore Durbar*
Aruna Roy	*The RTI Story: Power to the People*
Ashis Ray	*Laid to Rest: The Controversy of Subhas Chandra Bose's Death*
Bertil Falk	*Feroze: The Forgotten Gandhi*
Brij Mohan Bhalla	*Kasturba Gandhi: A Biography*
Devika Sethi	*Banned & Censored: What The British Raj Didn't Want Us To Read*
Harinder Baweja (Ed.)	*26/11 Mumbai Attacked*
Harinder Baweja	*A Soldier's Diary: Kargil – The Inside Story*
Ian H. Magedera	*Indian Videshinis: European Women in India*
Kunal Purandare	*Ramakant Achrekar: A Biography*
Lakshmi Subramanian	*Singing Gandhi's India: Music and Sonic Nationalism*
Maj. Gen. Ian Cardozo	*Param Vir: Our Heroes in Battle*
Moin Mir	*Surat: Fall of a Port, Rise of a Prince, Defeat of the East India Company in the House Of Commons*
Monisha Rajesh	*Around India in 80 Trains*
Noorul Hasan	*Meena Kumari: The Poet*
Rajika Bhandari	*The Raj on the Move: Story of the Dak Bungalow*
Ralph Russell	*The Famous Ghalib: The Sound of my Moving Pen*
Rahul Bedi	*The Last Word: Obituaries of 100 Indian who led Unusual Lives*
R.V. Smith	*Delhi: Unknown Tales of a City*
Salman Akthar	*The Book of Emotions*
Shrabani Basu	*Spy Princess: The Life of Noor Inayat Khan*
Shahrayar Khan	*Bhopal Connections: Vignettes of Royal Rule*
Shantanu Guha Ray	*Mahi: The Story of India's Most Successful Captain*
S. Hussain Zaidi	*Dongri to Dubai*
Sunil Gupta and Sunetra Choudhury	*Black Warrant: Confessions of a Tihar Jailer*
Thomas Weber	*Going Native: Gandhi's Relationship with Western Women*
Thomas Weber	*Gandhi at First Sight*
Vaibhav Purandare	*Sachin Tendulkar: A Definitive Biography*
Vappala Balachandran	*A Life in Shadow: The Secret Story of ACN Nambiar – A Forgotten Anti-Colonial Warrior*
Vir Sanghvi	*Men of Steel: India's Business Leaders in Candid Conversation*

The story of Delhi written by Bahadur Shah Zafar's grandson

Sawaneh-i Dehli

BIOGRAPHY OF DELHI

MIRZA AHMAD AKHTAR GORGANI

translated by

ATHER FAROUQUI

LOTUS COLLECTION

ROLI BOOKS

Lotus Collection

First published in 2023

The Lotus Collection
An imprint of
Roli Books Pvt. Ltd
M-75, Greater Kailash II Market, New Delhi 110 048
Phone: ++91 (011) 40682000
E-mail: info@rolibooks.com
Website: www.rolibooks.com
Also at Bengaluru, Chennai, & Mumbai

Layout Design: Bhagirath Kumar
Production: Lavinia Rao

ISBN: 978-93-92130-13-7

Typeset in Minion Pro by Roli Books Pvt. Ltd
Printed at Saurabh Printers Pvt. Ltd.

For Narayani Gupta and Swapna Liddle,
eminent historians of Delhi.

Contents

Translator's Note *ix*

Table of Discrepancies in the Years of Accession to the Throne and the Years of Death *xviii*

Table of Discrepancies in the Years of Construction *xx*

Preface *xxv*

1. Dehli 1
2. The Maharajas who Ruled over Dehli 17
3. A Brief Account of Muslim Monarchs 23
4. List of Kings who Sat on the Throne of Dehli 28
5. Story of the Muslim Rule in India from 588 AH [1192] to 1273 AH [1759] 32
6. The Decline and Ruin of the City of Dehli 40
7. An Account of Existing Monuments in Shahjahanabad, Dehli 58
8. The British at the Helm of India 68

Notes *75*

Translator's Note

Some events are so dramatic that any record of them appears like fiction. The life of Bahadur Shah Zafar, the last emperor of Delhi, and his family took such a drastic turn in 1857 that it seems beyond belief: from the Emperor of India (though admittedly mostly a figurehead one) to a prisoner in Rangoon (now Yangon), far from his beloved homeland. His life has generated numerous books, especially with the events of 1857 and Delhi in 1857, as a fulcrum; some are fictional and fanciful accounts. *Sawaneh-i Dehli* (A tale or biography of Delhi) is a creation of Mirza Ahmad Akhtar Gorgani (1840–1910). Born in the Red Fort, Akhtar Gorgani was the eldest son of Mohammad Dara Bakht Miran Shah (1790–1849), who was Bahadur Shah Zafar's eldest son and the Crown Prince.

When Akbar Shah Sani (Akbar II) passed away on 28 September 1837, Zafar ascended the throne in a ceremony conducted at the Red Fort at 3 a.m. No love was lost between the father and the son, and the question of succession had been a matter of strain for all the parties involved – Akbar II, Zafar and the East India Company. To avoid a similar tussle, at Resident Thomas Metcalfe's suggestion, Dara Bakht was declared the *wali ahd* (heir apparent) at the accession ceremony itself. Historians have suggested that Dara Bakht may not have been Zafar's first choice for his successor, as he preferred the second son Mirza Muhammad Shah Rukh. Shah Rukh was responsible for the palace's management and was appointed *vazir* in 1840. Be that as it may, Shah Rukh died in 1847 after contracting malaria during a hunting expedition in the *terai* region of the Himalayas. Two years later, his elder brother followed, dying of cough, cold and fever at the age of 57. The old perilous question of succession had returned.

After Dara Bakht's demise, at least some of his family moved out of the Fort and started living in the city of Shahjahanabad. The family continued to get an allowance from the Emperor till 1857. What happened to them after the Uprising is not known.

The common belief is that, after the events of 1857, the author of *Sawaneh-i Dehli* –Akhtar Gorgani – who was seventeen then, went underground and lived incognito in Kairana, a town near Meerut. We have no information about what he and his family did after arriving in Kairana, except in the form of hearsay and oral tradition. This lack of knowledge can largely be attributed to the violent retribution that was mounted against Zafar and the Mughal family by the British. Those who survived the violence lived in hiding and as far away from Delhi as possible. Therefore, details of the life of this book's author are hard to come by. After the Uprising, he led a peripatetic life for 20-25 years and practised Unani medicine. Prof. Hakim Syed Zillur Rahman, who has written an encyclopaedic book on the chief practitioners of Unani medicine in his *History of Unani Medicine in Dehli* (Translated into English by Zakaria Virk), gives a short biography of Akhtar Gorgani, which I am quoting in full here:

> He was the grandson of the last Mughal King, Bahadur Shah Zafar (d. 1862), and the younger brother of Mirza Dara Bakht Meeran Shah (d. 1849). [*This is incorrect since Dara Bakht was the son and not the grandson of Zafar.*] Dara Bakht was the crown prince of Bahadur Shah Zafar, but he died during Bahadur Shah's lifetime. Mirza Fakhru replaced him as the crown prince.
>
> He left Dehli in 1857 and spent the next 20-25 years in isolation for fear of detention. He lived in several cities in North India, including Bhopal. Finally, he settled in Kairana (Now in Shamli district of Western UP) and

operated a clinic there for many years. Through his books in medicine and Sufism and with help from his friends, Commissioner Dehli gave him a pension of Rs. 10/- monthly. In medicine, he was a disciple of Hakim Hassam ud-Din. He authored several treatises in medicine and Sufism. *Qarbabin-i-Sultani* is his magnum opus. In this treatise, he copied those prescriptions suggested for princes of Qila Mua'alla and of these, Mirza Akhtar had tested on himself. This book is in Persian and printed in 1889 at Mat'ba-i Mazhar al-Ajai'eb Dehli.

One of his treatises is in versed form *Elaj al-Huma ma'a Takmila wa qawai'd Nabaz.* At the request of Maulvi Hafez Muhammad Abd al-Ahad (owner of Matb'a Mujtaba'ee Dehli), it was printed at Mat'ba Mazhar al-Ajai'eb Dehli. According to the author of *Khumkhana-i Javid,* one of his books is *Sawaneh-i Dehli.*

Of his relatives in Kairana, my dear friend Tanveer Ahmad Alavi Kairanvi had seen Mirza Muhammad Shah and Mirza Masood Shah, who lived in Mohalla Khail Kilan. They lived in abject poverty. Mirza Muhammad Shah operated a 'Panwari' (betel-seller) shop. He had no property; their houses were dilapidated. There were coarse curtains on the doors, and women donned veils.

Legend has it that after his passing, Akhtar Gorgani's belongings included the manuscript of this book, which exposed the secret that the deceased was a prince. The manuscript was supposedly a secret document detailing the events of 1857. While this fable has been circulating in India and Pakistan by word of mouth, it appears patently concocted after one has studied the book. Kairana is about 100 km from Delhi, parallel to the Yamuna River, and Meerut is about 30 km east of the Yamuna, roughly equidistant from Delhi and Kairana. It is unlikely that anyone close to the family of Bahadur Shah Zafar could remain incognito in Kairana after 1857. Traditionally, Meerut Cantonment was known to be the first to rise in revolt – although some historians believe it was Ambala where the revolt first broke out. Whatever may be the case, the soldiers who first reached Delhi were from Meerut Cantonment and the smallest villages in and around Meerut, and, of course, Delhi were then infested with British spies.

The author has used 'Gorgani' after his name and after the names of his father, Dara Bakht, and of the last emperor, Bahadur Shah Zafar (1775–1862). Gorgani, or Gorkani, was a title for Amir Timur (1336–1405), also known as Tamerlane. Babur (1483–1530), the great-great-grandson of Tamerlane, founded the Mughal dynasty. It is interesting to note that G*organi* is a Turkish word meaning son-in-law. The title was given to Tamerlane and the future kings of his dynasty because they often married Turkish women. To the translator's knowledge, Gorgani was never used as a title for Bahadur Shah Zafar or any of the Mughal emperors. While

Dara Bakht was indeed first in line for the throne of Delhi, his children, after his death, were nowhere close to being contenders to the throne. Mirza Ahmad Akhtar seems to have adopted the title Gorgani to elevate his father's stature and, indeed, his own to that of the emperor.

I have not studied the revolt of 1857 and its aftermath in great depth, and I am not fortunate enough to count myself a student of history. However, I have had the chance to translate books relating to the period, which has provided me with some knowledge of the circumstances surrounding the event. It is, therefore, possible to surmise after reading the text that the author may have settled in Kairana with the consent of the British. Perhaps also that the British endorsed his wish to pen this tract. The subservient tone in which he has described British officials supports this observation.

When the 150th anniversary of 1857 was observed in 2007, there was a buzz about the First War of Independence. In academia, 1857 became a theme for all kinds of writings and speeches, more so because the government had loosened its purse strings to celebrate the event. The present work was 'discovered' around this time. Possibly no one translated the entire tract, but it was much talked about. Extracts from it were used in newspaper writings.

The Mughals – particularly the later Mughals – are much maligned characters of Indian history, particularly in the twenty-first century. If the earlier Mughals are traduced as anti-Hindu tyrants, the later ones are routinely derided as powerless, pleasure-seeking and hedonistic. However, they were not quite what they are believed to be. The Mughals, to the very last, were highly intelligent, cultured and sophisticated. It is a British fiction that since the later Mughals were no good, a vacuum was created that the East India Company was obliged to step in and fill. Such histories cannot be taken seriously. It is also unfortunate that many accounts of 1857 have been generated by writers who do not have even basic training in history. This has further added to the fiction around 1857 and related events.

The author of *Sawaneh-i Dehli* knew very little of history, as a reader may reasonably surmise from the footnotes included with this translation. The author often gives Hijri dates in the text, except in the last chapter. A facsimile of the 1894 book is preserved in the library of Jamia Millia Islamia. It is in a decrepit condition and illegible in several places. Apart from guesswork, I had to rely on the Urdu Academy's text because that was, in all likelihood, based on the Hardinge Library text, though it is not mentioned anywhere. Delhi Urdu Academy books on Delhi published in the early years after its establishment in 1981 were primarily copies of Hardinge Library originals. The Delhi Urdu Academy republished these books without considering the rules of textual criticism, which must be followed in any compilation.

In that period, a person called 'Bahar' Allahabadi was

probably in charge of the Urdu Section at the library. Now it is virtually impossible to benefit from any book in that library. Over the last many years, books and manuscripts have been pushed into jute bags, as I last witnessed in September 2021. Moreover, there are such strict rules about accessing manuscripts that it is well-nigh impossible to lay one's hands on them. Media reports have suggested that the library's dire straits owe to a severe financial crunch.

I managed to access the text of 1894 through Dr Shaista Bedar, Director of the Khudabaksh Oriental Public Library of Patna, who made a digital copy available from the library of Jamia Millia Islamia in virtually no time. When I contacted the Jamia library on my own, the computerized catalogue mentioned only the Urdu Academy text, but I got this invaluable text quite quickly through Dr Bedar's kindness. I want to express my immense gratitude to her. I am also grateful to Ms Shazia Alvi, Assistant Librarian of Jamia Millia Islamia Library, for her help. To the best of my knowledge, this edition is not available in any important library where access to the internet is possible. A gentleman owning a private collection in Kairana claimed to have this edition but never gave me a facsimile copy of the cover page, though I left no stone unturned in pursuing this lead.

After completing the translation and including footnotes a few years ago, I thought it would be good to have the expertise of a medieval Indian historian on board. Ms Riya

Gupta, a research scholar at the Jawaharlal Nehru University (JNU), agreed to come to my aid. After looking over the translation, she suggested several amendments, which I followed. I am grateful for her generosity and help. This is a new translation based on the text from the library of Jamia Millia Islamia.

I am also grateful to Baidar Bakht, who is very well-versed in the history of Delhi and its traditional culture, for reviewing my translation. I am incredibly grateful to Nikhil Kumar for his valuable suggestions and wish to dedicate my next book on Delhi to him.

Ather Farouqui
March 2023
New Delhi

Table of Discrepancies in the Years of Accession to the Throne and the Years of Death[1]

Sl. No.	Detail/Incidents	Entry of *Sawaneh-i Dehli*		Entry of *Aasar-us Sanadeed*	
		Year of accession to the throne	Year of death	Year of accession to the throne	Year of death
1	Sultana Razia	634 AH [1236]	---	633 AH [1235]	---
2	Naseeruddin Mahmood or Sultan Nasiruddin Mahmood Shah	644 AH [1246]	---	634 AH [1236]	---
3	Shahabuddin Umar [According to *Sawaneh-i Dehli*], or Shahabuddin [According to *Aasar-us Sanadeed*]	--- ---	--- 717 AH [1317]		--- Nothing is entered
4	Qutubuddin Mubarak Shah	716 AH [1316]	---	717 AH [1317]	---
5	Sultan Nasiruddin Khusroo Khan	721 AH [1321]	721 AH [1321]	720 AH [1320]	720 AH [1320]
6	Ghayasuddin Tughlaq	720 AH [1320]	---	721 AH [1321]	---
7	Abu Bakr Shah	---	793 AH [1391]	---	792 AH [1289]

8	Nasiruddin Mahmood Shah [According to *Aasar-us Sanadeed*], or Mahmood Shah [According to *Sawaneh-i Dehli*]	816 AH [1413]	---	---	815 AH [1412]
9	Khizr Khan	816 AH [1413]	---	817 AH [1414]	---
10	Muhammad Shah	---	847 AH [1443]	---	849 AH [1445]
11	Alauddin	847 AH [1443]	883 AH [1478]	849 AH [1445]	852 AH [1448] (Removed) 855 AH [1451] (Demise)
12	Bahlul Lodi	852 AH [1448]	---	855 AH [1451]	---
13	Sikandar Lodi	---	914 AH [1508]	---	923 AH [1517]
14	Shahabuddin Muhammad Shahjahan	1048 AH [1638]	---	1000 AH [1591]	---
15	Bahadur Shah Sani	---	1277 AH [1860] (Removed) 1279 AH [1862] (Demise)		There is no year mentioned

1. This table was not part of the original text but was compiled by Marghub Abidi.

Table of Discrepancies in the Years of Construction

Sl. No.	Name of the Building	Year of Construction (in *Sawaneh-i Dehli*)	Year of Construction (In *Aasar-us Sanadeed*)
1	Jama Masjid	1066 AH [1655]	1060 AH [1650]
2	Masjid Fatehpuri	The date of construction is not mentioned.	1060 AH [1650]
3	Zeenat ul Masajid	1112 AH [1700]	1122 AH [1710]
4	Masjid Dariba Kalan	1115 AH [1903]	1135 AH [1722]
5	Kali Masjid		772 AH [1322]
6	Dargah Shah Turkman Bayabani	958 AH [1551]	638 AH [1240]
7	Girja Ghar	1266 AH [1849]	1242 AH [1826]
8	Neeli Chatri		939 AH [1532]
9	Jain Mandir Dharampur (In *Sawaneh-i Dehli*), or Jainiyon ka Bada Mandir in *Aasar-us Sanadeed*		1215 AH [1800]
10	Bagh Roshan Ara		1064 AH [1653]
11	Bagh Qudsia		1162 AH [1749]
12	Saleem Gadh [Garh]	958 AH [1551]	1031 AH [1621]

13	Jog Maya	1233 AH [1817]	1243 AH [1827]
14	Dargah Hazrat Nizamuddin	It was constructed several times	725 AH [1325]
15	Maqbara Sultan Ghazi		629 AH [1231]
16	Dargah Hazrat Syed Hasan Rasool Numa	778 AH [1376]	1103 AH [1691]
17	Gumbad Taga Khan		974 AH [1566]
18	Jharna Qutub Sahab (According to *Sawaneh-i Dehli*), or Jharna (According to *Aasar-us Sanadeed*)	1143 AH [1730]	1112 AH [1700]
19	Chausanth Khamba		1034 AH [1624]
20	Arab Sarae	958 AH [1551]	968 AH [1560]
21	Mehjar Jahan Ara Begum	1054 AH [1644]	1092 AH [1681]
22	Maqbara Humayun Badshah		937 AH [1530]
23	Maqbara Tughlaq	726 AH [1325]	725 AH [1325]
24	Maqbara Ghayasuddin	725 AH [1325]	882 AH [1477]
25	Masjid Esa Khan	954 AH [1547]	984 AH [1576]
26	Maqbara Khan Khana		1036 AH [1626]

27	Jail Khana Delhi (According to *Sawaneh-i Dehli*), or Jail Khana yah Sarai (According to *Aasar-us Sanadeed*)	---	1017 AH [1608] ----
28	Moth ki Masjid	909 AH [1503]	894 AH [1488]
29	Maqbara Safdar Jung	1060 AH [1650]	1167 AH [1753]
30	Qila Hazar Sutoon	90 AH [708]	728 AH [1327]
31	Qila Tughlaq (According to *Sawaneh-i Dehli*) or Qila Tuqhlaqabad according to *Aasar-us Sanadeed.*	---	723 AH [1323] ---
32	Dargah Shaikh Salahuddin	752 AH [1351]	754 AH [1353]
33	Kotla Firoz Shah	775 AH [1373]	755 AH [1354]
34	Qutub Minar	616 AH [1291]	538 AH [1143]
35	Sher Mandal	950 AH [1543]	848 AH [1444]
36	Dargah Imam Zamin	1044 AH [1634]	Even before 944 AH [1537]
37	Maqbara Sultan Sikandar Lodi	775 AH [1373]	923 AH [1517]

1. This table was not part of the original text but was compiled and added by Marghub Abidi.

The Original Title Page in Urdu

Sawāniḥ -i Dehlī

A complete record of past and present unfortunate events

Authored and compiled by

Honourable Prince Mirza Ahmed Akhtar Gorgani
The eldest son of Mirza Dara Bakht Miran Shah
Crown Prince of Abu Zafar Sirajuddin Muhammad
Bahadur Shah Zafar
(The last Mughal Emperor of India)

On Request of
N. Dasi Sahib, Near Dariba Kalan, Delhi

Published by
Matba-i Iftekhar Delhi in 1894

Verses of the Holy Quran (illegible)

Preface

(In the name of Allah, most gracious and most compassionate)

All praise to Thee, the Almighty, from the very depth of my heart and Thou art, full of mercy and compassion, who endowed light to stars and vast expanses above; turned the fire into a floral bed for Abraham, making all express their gratitude to the Creator. He, full of majesty and honour, led Moses to the path of righteousness and made him a prophet, causing the downfall of vicious Nimrod and Pharaoh and condemning them to the abyss of the fire of hell. It is the wisdom of the Omnipotent which lights the flame of the sun, which dispels all-round darkness, and His miracle of providing nourishment to man and all the creatures under the sun, followed by the cycle of days and nights, and the golden light of the moon (removing nocturnal darkness).

Without a doubt, no partner has He
Unique, alone, all alone
Listener, seer, knower, omniscient
All powerful, beyond all domains
Generous bestower of mercy
Praiseworthy, all-beholding, exalted, wise
Blessed, taking care of all, and bestower of favours
Praiseworthy
Comprehending, wisest of all Creator of time, foreknowing
Free of blemish and above reproach.

The source of the warmth of my speech is the inspirational light of the prophethood of the great one who, merely by the waving of his index finger, can split the moon into two, and by the grace of whom sinners are spared from the eternal fire of hell chastisement. By the grace of the miracle of his light and splendour has dawned the enlightenment of the entire creation, and the doors of the mercy of Allah opened up… that imparted meaning and content into the purposefulness of Allah's creation:

Prophet Muhammad (Peace be upon him) is mercy for the world
I am a slave of his very name
There is no one else being his equal
The beloved who is loyal to the lover
Perfect in deport and bearing
Unique much as his body casts no shadow
A holy light personified in self
Keeping all enthralled by his beauty.

After paying this due obeisance to the Mercy of the Worlds, and to his companions, this humble self, Mirza Ahmad Akhtar Chishti Fakhri, the eldest son of Muhammad Dara Bakht Miran Shah, the crown prince of Hazrat Abu Zafar Sirajuddin Muhammad Bahadur Shah Zafar, currently dwelling in the town of Kairana, in the district of Muzaffarnagar, prays for his parents and ancestors, that they be in peace in the eternal world.

After completing the book *Mujarrabāt-i Sultānī,* this poor, displaced and deserted soul has written this modest book in order to make his sons – Mirza Muhammad Shah, Mirza Mahmud Shah and Mirza Masud Shah – briefly aware [of events and trends], and titled it *Sawanih-i Dehli.* As such, readers are urged to overlook any inaccuracies or errors that might have inadvertently crept in.

Given His grace, nothing is hard to accomplish.

Dehli[1]

In the ancient texts scribed by old Indian historians, Dehli is described as an ancient and holy city which was the abode of the gods, a sacred spot where Lord Indra celebrated an event known as Rahas, for merry-making, along with fellow gods. According to *Dilli Mahatam*, Dehli is a holy city and a pilgrimage centre for Indians, like Benaras, Allahabad and Haridwar, among others; and gods, like in many other [sacred] places, live here. By gods are meant the dwellers of the heavens. As mentioned in the book, many hallowed saints dwelt and performed their rituals of worship here. Living and dying in Dehli was supposed to be a blessing. A few miles from the city is the spot where the great sage Vishwamitra used to live, pray and worship. The site was earlier known as Prabhashkund but has now become known as Surajkund. However, the settlement around was known as Sohna. The same town later came to be called Indraprastha, after Lord Indra, the highest-ranking among the gods. Thus the original name of Dehli was Indraprastha. It attained great popularity and hence was known as Sohna, meaning lovely. Afterwards, Sohna has been translated as Dilli, meaning heart-touching. Some people say that Dehli was named after the ruler Raja Dalpal while others say that it gets its name from a marshland (*dal-dal*), but it is situated on a hilly tract. Be that as it may, the city's population now comprises the old and the new, and according to some estimates, its territory now extends over a total length of 12 to 13 *kos* and a width of 5 to 6 *kos*.[2] Moreover, an area extending over some 500 *kos* is known as Dilli Mandal Des.

Dehli being an old and revered place, the Pandavas had shifted their capital to the city from Hastinapur. Unfortunately, the Hindus did not correctly document their history. Therefore it is hard to talk with any certainty about Dehli's foundation and its early inhabitation. It is also difficult to ascertain this ancient city's exact age. However, the buildings that are still in existence – and the ruins of several others – reveal that it is one of the oldest cities in the Indian subcontinent and the world. The old fort used to be called Inderpat during the days of the Hindu rulers. In Sher Shah's time, it came to be known as Shergarh, and during Humayun's reign, it became Din Panah. Thus it acquired several names across epochs. According to legend, certain buildings were erected during the time of Emperor Ashoka, who ruled around 332BC[3] in Magadh. After that, there were many modifications in the locations and names given to Dehli, but no authentic account is available. That was a dark age in the annals of history.

Still, some history books confirm that long after the Pandavas and Kauravas, Raja Anangpal Tomar built a city and a fort in the year 1223 in his name. Later, in 580 AH (1184), Raja Prithviraj [Chauhan] built a fortress, a palace, an orchard, and a leisure retreat, whose remains are still evident in the village of Mehrauli. His palace and place of worship have survived till this time. According to several historians, it was Prithviraj who built the first storey of Qutub Minar in order to perform his daily ritual of worshipping the rising sun before taking his first meal of the day.[4] Notably, Qutub Minar is a famous monument in Dehli and across the entire country.

The invasions of Shihabuddin [Muhammad] Ghori led to the advent of Islam in India. The joint forces of Prithviraj and other Hindu kings repulsed the first massive invasion in the year 587 AH [1191] at Tarawadi[5] [modern-day Taraori]. But the invader returned the following year with a much larger force at his command, resulting in the Hindu rajas' downfall on the same battlefield. Khande Rao, known for his exceptional gallantry and courage, was killed, and Prithviraj was taken prisoner on the banks of Saraswati River.[6] Thus, the absolute downfall of Hindu rulers and chieftains began. The Muslim success at Tarawadi shook the very foundations of Hindu power. After that, they were fated to lose sovereignty, power, and supremacy for all time to come and could never flourish again. In the year 589 AH [1194], the defeat of Jai Chand, a cousin brother of Prithviraj, drove the final nail in the coffin of Hindu rule in India.

Ghori himself chose to return home after handing over the reins of governance to Qutbuddin Aibak, his favourite slave, to rule India on his behalf. This led to the foundation of the Sultanate of Dehli, with Qutbuddin as the first ruler of the Slave dynasty. Following his demise, his son Aram Shah took over for a brief period but being addicted to a life of ease and luxury, he proved to be an incapable ruler and was deposed. Turkish chiefs then chose Shamsuddin Altamash [also Iltutmish], a talented slave of Aibak, to take over the reins of the Sultanate. Altamash being pious, wise and efficient, proved to be a benign ruler. He introduced numerous schemes for the welfare of the people and took up campaigns for further expansion and consolidation of the new empire. He also built the famous Qutub Minar in Dehli, naming it after his mentor Qutbuddin Aibak.

Later, internal strife and internecine quarrels caused instability and unrest until Sultan Nasiruddin Mahmud took over the sultanate's reins in 644 AH [1246]. His was a period of overall prosperity for the subjects. His wise and capable minister Ghiyasuddin Balban played an active role in governance. Balban organized the whole state and remarkably improved the conditions in Dehli's capital. He named Dehli Marzghan.[7] During those times, several princes and [deposed] rulers from Central Asian states arrived in Dehli and sought refuge to escape the terror of the Mongols – the clan of Genghis Khan, the great conqueror of his time. Balban got the refugee princes settled in different parts of Dehli and created space for them by establishing localities and colonies under their names.[8]

In 684 AH [1287], Kaiqobad founded a beautiful and vast new city on the banks of Yamuna River named Kilokheri.[9] This township was perhaps situated in the vicinity of Humayun's tomb as it stands today. Since the tomb of Kaiqobad is located there and because (apparently) he was laid to rest in his palace itself, it can be concluded that Kilokheri was located there. After the assassination of Kaiqobad, the reins of the sultanate passed from the Slave dynasty to the Khaljis. The first sultan of the Khalji dynasty, Jalaluddin Khalji, handed over the affairs of the state to his nephew, Alauddin Khalji, and took to a life of ease and leisure. But Jalaluddin Khalji was later assassinated, and following his death, Alauddin

Khalji formally crowned himself sultan. He soon invaded and conquered several states in the Deccan region of India. He gathered a lot of wealth from the conquered areas and spent it lavishly. He further renovated the city of Kaushak Mahal, making it a place of grandeur. He also built a grand fort and a palace named Kaushak-i Sabz. But he was not a good administrator and spent much time in dalliance with his beloved, Koladevi Rani. Like him, his son Khizr Khan too whiled away his time with his much-loved companion Deval Devi. The overall outcome of this incompetence and licentiousness spelt the doom of the Khaljis and paved the way for the advent of the Tughlaq dynasty.[10]

Sultan Ghiyasuddin Tughlaq Shah[11] founded the city of Tughlaqabad (House of the Tughlaqs) in 724 AH (1324) and built a formidable fort, completed in the reign of his son and successor, Sultan Moizuddin alias Juna Shah. Juna Shah [Muhammad bin Tughlaq] also built a magnificent palace of his own which contained a thousand pillars.[12] He built many other buildings of solid rock as well.[13] The city eventually fell casualty to the impermanence that is the only permanence in this world. However, the fort, known as Tughlaqabad, still stands in a crumbling state as a grim reminder of the vagaries of time.

Of all the rulers of the Tughlaq dynasty, Firoze Shah Tughlaq was the one who ushered in prosperity and plenitude to his kingdom. Along with economic prosperity, he also took steps to promote art and culture, instituting awards of merit for poets and scholars of the time. In 755 AH (1354), he built a magnificent city on the banks of the Yamuna. In the following year, i.e., 756 AH (1355), he ordered the digging of a canal from Satluj River [in present-day Punjab] to Jhajjar [in present-day Haryana]. Another canal was dug from the Yamuna to Hansi and Hissar [in present-day Haryana] in 757 AH (1356). Firoze Shah also built a new fort named Hissar-e Firoza.

Additionally, he got an underground tank constructed and had it connected to a canal. A smaller canal was dug from Khaggar, brought to Hissar Sarasti [in present-day Haryana], and extended beyond. The same year was celebrated grandly to commemorate the creation of a new city named Firozabad.[14] Traces of this old city can still be seen. An iconic pillar, sacred for Hindus, was brought by the functionaries of the government from central India [actually present-day Haryana] and was installed near the city.[15] An imposing mansion was built to surround the pillar, along with a grand mosque, the minarets of which are still standing. The steel pillar is known as Firoze Shah ki Laat or Kotle ki Laat, which inspired the famous poet Insha to pen the following verse:

> Several days have gone by, so let us again go
> To the fourth (upper) part of the pillar of Firoze Shah.[16]

After Firoze Shah's death, internal strife and conflict weakened the empire's foundations. During Mahmud Tughlaq's reign in 801 AH [1398], the great and gracious ancestor of this writer, Amir Timur, arrived in India and stayed in Dehli for a while. Mahmud Tughlaq fled to Gujarat. As a result, the city of Dehli was left to its fate in the face of the vast invading army. Nevertheless, Mahmud returned to Dehli once Timur departed but died within a year or two. In the meantime, Sayyid Khizr Khan, the governor of Multan, declared himself the vice-regent of Timur and ascended to the throne as Sultan. However, devastating quarrels significantly weakened his kingdom, and his area of influence did not extend beyond a few *kos*, while the other provinces were under his control only in name. Later, Khizr Khan's son and successor, Sayyid Mubarak Shah, built a fort named Mubarakabad. Still, during his grandson's tenure, the entire kingdom passed out of the hands of the Sayyids.[17] And then rose the Lodis, who founded the Lodi dynasty.

The first Lodi sultan, Bahlol Lodi, restored the glory of Dehli somewhat by retaining it as his capital. However, his son and successor, Sikandar Lodi, moved the capital to Agra and ruled from there until 997 AH (1589),[18] depriving Dehli of the status of the royal capital. Sikandar's son and successor, Ibrahim Lodi, proved to be a ruthless tyrant and, as a result, at the invitation of the governor of Multan, Daulat Khan, the great king Zahiruddin Babur, king of kings and ancestor of the writer of this book, invaded India. He cut through the columns of the army of Ibrahim Lodi in 932 AH [1526] in a fierce battle at Panipat [in present-day Haryana]. He emerged victorious and occupied Dehli. Henceforth, the Mughal injunction ran far and wide in the real sense. A new currency was issued, and a proclamation (*khutba*) was made that a new emperor, Babur, had come to administer India. Poetically, it was documented in history in these words:

> Zahiruddin Muhammad Shah Babur
> Of the munificence of Alexander[19] and the might of Bahram[20]
> Conquered the land of India
> Following an absolute conquest
> The event is recorded in verse form.

After a few years, Nasiruddin Muhammad Humayun ascended the throne, with Agra as his capital, but Dehli still stood apart prominently. Soon after, the Afghan chieftain Sher Shah Suri began invading the Mughal territory and forced Emperor Humayun to flee to Iran. Sher Shah made Dehli his capital and rebuilt the old fort, renaming it Shergarh. A new complex came up along the banks of Yamuna River under Sher Shah's son Salim Shah. He built a strong citadel, naming it Salimgarh. Other structures built by him included a step-well (*Khārībā'olī*)[21] and a mosque at a place now known as

Lahori Gate. Soon his dominion ran into trouble, and, by the grace of Allah, Emperor Humayun returned to re-establish his rule in India. He carried out certain reforms,[22] enhanced the look of the fort and gave it the magnificent name of Din Panah. Unfortunately, within a year, he died, bringing the young Jalaluddin Muhammad Akbar to the throne. Akbar ascended the throne at Kalanaur in present-day Punjab. After routing the forces of Hemu at Panipat in 962 AH [1555],[23] he decimated the Afghan elements altogether. In his reign, Agra was restored to its old glory and made the capital in preference to Dehli, and so it remained till the reign of the majestic and revered Shahabuddin Muhammad Shah Jahan. This magnificent monarch started restoring the glory of the city of Dehli only in the twelfth year of his rule. It could aptly be said that he re-laid the foundations of the city. Various Mughal emperors dotted the empire with imposing towns and cities, each of rare excellence.

The city of Dehli is spread over a radius of 7 miles and encompasses magnificent palaces and mansions which house the nobility and other dignitaries. After that, the fort was constructed, whose majesty and beauty remain unrivalled under the sun. It took ten years of tireless labour and gigantic amounts of money to build the fort and a new city complex. A poetic date for record in verse was pronounced, which ran as follows and is equivalent to 1058 AH [1648]:

Shah Jahan became the emperor
From the city of Shahjahanabad.

The city, however, would have remained unprotected and imperfect without a boundary wall, and thus, in the year 1060 AH (1650), a boundary wall of bricks and mortar was built at an expenditure of Rs 1.5 lakh. But it soon caved in and fell in the rainy season. In the year 1061 AH (1651), it was replaced with a more durable wall of solid stone and rock, 6610 yards long, 4 yards wide, and 9 yards high. Its cost came to Rs 3.5 lakh.[24] The city had twelve gates, four large windows, fifty-six watchtowers, and 168 ramparts and fortresses for the troops to stand guard against any possible attack by an enemy. Some of them have survived; among them are Dehli Gate, Turkman Gate, Ajmeri Gate, Lahori Gate, Kashmiri Gate, Nigambodh Gate, and Rajghat Gate. While the boundaries of Mori Gate and Phoota Gate remain, the gates themselves have crumbled. There is also no trace of Kabuli Gate and other gates. Among the windows, one at Farash Khana and another at Masjid Ghat survive,[25] but the rest have vanished. However, Calcutta Gate, built by the last emperor [Bahadur Shah Zafar], is still intact.

Nehr-i Faiz, a canal at Parganah Safedun [in present-day Haryana] dating back to the reign of Firoze Shah Tughlaq, was extended at the behest of Emperor Akbar, under the supervision of Shihabuddin, one of his chiefs in Dehli. It was renamed Nehr-e Shahab. Due to disuse, it fell into ruin until yet another chief, Ali Mardan Khan, performed extensive repairs on it to win Emperor Shah Jahan's favour. The canal reached the palaces and flowed through Hayat Baksh Bagh, the garden inside the fort.[26] One can still see its remains, but its water no longer reaches the fort.

Emperor Alamgir [Aurangzeb] took forward the expansion of the capital and constructed many new buildings, further adding to the charm of the city. Hence, there was a large influx of people from different provinces into the capital. There was no looking back, and the city's splendour magnified manifold.

Dehli's climate is moderate throughout the year and during all seasons. The city is situated at 800 feet[27] above sea level, and its atmosphere is salubrious for the inhabitants. But perhaps a city that was the pride of the world and challenged the beauty of paradise fell victim to its retributive acts and the vicissitudes of time. One may say that the glory of the city of enchantments itself led it on to the path of destruction:

> Natural resplendence became its undoing.[28]

Foreign invasions, aided by internal disputes and internecine quarrels, caused Dehli's downfall. The attacks by Nadir Shah and Ahmad Shah Abdali, coupled with the devastation caused by the Marathas, culminated in the tragic events of 1857. The destruction can be measured by the fact that the population of twenty lakh people in the capital shrank to just 1.93 lakh, according to the census of 1891. In addition, many smaller towns and hundreds of villages on the periphery of Dehli remained sparsely inhabited:

> See what a contrast![29]

Yet, notwithstanding the devastation, Dehli continued to exude charm and splendour, captivating the hearts of the people who were willing to wager anything for just a glimpse of it; so deeply was its glorious image engraved on the collective memory of the populace. Thus, there was no shortage of connoisseurs of archaeology and archives visiting the city regularly, and there are, of course, historians and other scholars coming in droves.

However, this is not all that Dehli has to offer. It is also famed as a centre of mysticism and an abode of pious saints. People come to pay their respects at the holy mausoleums of [Muslim and Hindu] saints like Khwaja Qutbuddin Bakhtiar Kaki, Hazrat Shah Turkman Biyabani, Hazrat Sultan Nizamuddin Aulia, Hazrat Khwaja Nasiruddin Mahmud Chirag Dehlvi, Hazrat Amir Khusrau, Shaikh Shihabuddin Aashiq, Khuda Mulk, Kabir ul Aulia, Shaikh Salahuddin, Khwaja Mahmud Bahar, Shaikh Abdullah Qureshi, Shaikh Namshuddin Avtaar, Sayyid Hasan

Rasulnuma, Hazrat Maulana Fakhruddin Chishti Nizami, Hazrat Shaikh Muhammad Sabri, Hazrat Shah Bade Sahab Shamgarh, Baba Madhavdas Bairagi, and Bu Ali Qalandar Panipati.[30]

It was in keeping with Dehli's enviable repute that Lord Lytton, the Viceroy, held the grand court (*badā darbār*) in this city in 1877 to mark the assumption of the title of *Qaisar-i Hind* by Her Majesty, Queen Victoria. The rulers and courtiers of various states were honoured by being invited to attend the magnificent court.

I, the writer of this book, met a saintly ascetic somewhere in the mountainous region of northern India. He was indeed a savant, old and wise. In the course of my conversation with him, I asked him: What was the reason for the city to have suffered so many ravages, so many ups and downs, expansions and contractions during its ageless existence? I also asked why other cities in the world [even capitals] had not undergone such large-scale devastation while this city of ours had to go through so many periodical ravages.

He listened attentively before giving his well-considered answer. He maintained that Dehli was a sacred and sanctified city where the gods would descend and where saints and mystics of unquestionable piety would appear from time to time.

I further asked him: Was this city founded at some ill-omened time that led to its becoming cursed? He replied that its quality of holiness attracted so many heavenly persons who, once they had descended here, found that the city was also a place where acts of sin were committed. Angered by this, these holy people cursed the city.[31]

Not convinced, I pointed out that evil doings were also found in other holy places like Kashi, Prayag and Haridwar, but no devastation was seen there. He replied that the difference between these places and Dehli was that the latter was a capital. Thus, it called for instant retribution for anybody daring to defile it with sin. He said, 'It is the navel and the centre of the country, very much like your Kaaba, where one gets rewarded munificently for a righteous act and penalized manifold for corrupt acts. Dehli holds much the same rank in holiness, and when lechery and evil cross the barriers, one calamity or another is bound to occur in the city.' In verse, we could say:

> Fabulous as well as degraded we are![32]

Now the fort lies in ruins, the city is barren; the markets are deserted. For the old residents, there is nothing left to do here except shed copious tears, while those of the new generation keep wondering in disbelief:

> We have lost both the worlds,
> We belong nowhere, neither here nor there.[33]

Dehli is now a prominent centre of trade and commerce, yet its people yearn for plenty and prosperity:

Dehli was the choicest place in the world
The crème de la crème lived there
The wrath of the heavens fell on it and destroyed it
To that ruined place, we belong.[34]

The Maharajas who Ruled over Dehli*

Shri Maharaja Judhistar [Yudhishthir] is a sacrosanct name in the Puranas of a king who sat on the throne of Dehli during Paryug, i.e. 2687 BC. He was a sagacious and just ruler whose reign lasted for 128 years. However, he left this terrestrial abode and took his place in paradise at the advent of Kalyug. Raja Kashi Makh was the last ruler of the dynasty when an enormous convulsion shook the realm revolving around the betrayal of the raja at the hands of his minister Bisarwa, who proclaimed himself monarch of the kingdom thereafter.

The family of this Raja Bisarwa ruled for 502 years and

20 days, in the course of which it threw up as many as fifteen kings. Pratmalin was the last ruler of the family, and he too met his death at the hands of his minister – an usurper calling himself Raja Birban. That dynasty ruled for 423 years, 6 months and 23 days, with Raja Adhat being the last ruler.

Raja Adhat was given to a life of comfort and licence; as such, he allowed his minister to rule on his behalf. Another tale of betrayal, treachery and murder followed as his minister overthrew the debauch. He came to be known as Raja Dhinendra, and his dynasty ruled all for 333 years, 4 months and 15 days. The family produced nine rulers, with Raja Jaipal being the last of them – a callous and unjust king causing widespread discontent among rich and poor alike.

This resulted in an opportunity for the governor of Kumaon to launch an assault on Dehli. After a brief encounter, he took over the throne of Dehli, calling himself Maharaja Pagwanth (Raja Sukhwant, according to some). He ruled efficiently for fourteen years, following which greed and avarice tempted him to establish his writ through force and violent means. He dismissed and demoted his immediate aides indiscriminately and committed untold atrocities upon his subjects. This proved to be his undoing. Maharaja Bikramajit came to Dehli from Ujjain, his capital, and set things right. A minor conflict ensued, and the Maharaja proclaimed Dehli his new capital. He put his younger brother Raja Bharatrihari in charge of Ujjain.

Bikramajit ruled with justice and fairness for 93 years but fell to the intrigues of Samandarpal Yogi, and took his abode in paradise. The dynasty ended for the king had died without issue. There was no heir apparent and his brother Raja Bharatrihari opted for a life of asceticism, joining the Gorakhnath sect.

Now a word about Samandarpal Yogi, who made his way to the throne by sheer deceit and guile, proclaiming himself Raja Samandarpal Yogi. He generously distributed high offices and positions to his followers and fellow mendicants. He is described in ancient books on India's history. As many as sixteen members of his family ascended to the throne, spreading over 372 years, 1 month, and 20 days. The last of them, Raja Bikrampal, was particularly evil – avaricious and unjust. He invaded the Kingdom of Bharuch, which was then ruled by Raja Trilok Chand, a warrior known for his bravery and daring. The two armies met in bloody combat in which Raja Bikrampal was killed, and Raja Trilok Chand emerged the victor. As the enemy surrendered, a lot of treasure and ammunition fell into his hands.

While the Raja appointed his minister to govern Bharuch on his behalf, Raja Tilokchand took over the throne of Dehli. The Trilok Chand family ruled for 109 years and 27 days in all, with ten rulers following one after another – the last of them being Maharani Somwanti, who remained unmarried. She was the daughter of Gobind Chandra. She died within a year of becoming queen. There was no heir apparent, and a well-meaning group of ministers decided to anoint one Prem of the priestly order to the throne. The populace welcomed his appointment, and he ruled for 49 years, 11 months and 10 days as Raja Harprem. Three members of his dynasty ruled after him, and the family ruled for 93 years in all. The last to rule was Raja Mahapatra, whose reputation as a broad-minded man of high moral fibre evoked the envy of Raja Dahi Sen, who came from Bengal to invade Dehli with a large army contingent.

Raja Mahapatra, however, was a god-fearing person and hated bloodshed. He felt no particular attraction to pelf and power, and thus he opted for voluntary abdication from the throne. Despite the fact that he took to the path of mendicancy, Raja Dahi Sen did not rest content and took Raja Mahapatra prisoner and had him killed. According to some, the house of Dahi Sen reigned for 140 years, 2 months and 29 days with 13 rulers, the last being Damodar Sen.

During the latter's reign, the overlord of a hilly state conquered Dehli and ascended to the throne. He is known in history as Maharaja Deep Singh. This dynasty ruled for about 650 years, its last king being Raja Prithviraj, aka Pithora, who ascended to the throne in 1141. Dehli and Ajmer Sharif were both his capitals for the forty years of his rule. However, internal squabbling ultimately led to uncertainty – and therein lay the opportunity for Sultan Shahabuddin to enter India via Ghazni. However, this attempt met with failure, followed by ten further attempts, one after another. This was a prelude to fierce encounters between the two, resulting in heavy casualties. Till this time, despite deep dissensions, all the chieftains and more minor rulers used to pay formal obeisance before the throne of Dehli. But the rot had sunk in quite deep, and thus the Sultan-in-waiting, Shahabuddin, got his eleventh chance to launch an assault on Dehli. It resulted in the rout of Prithviraj, whose troops were already exhausted under the stress of repeated wars; no other king bothered to come to his help.

As a result, the Sultan emerged victorious, and Maharaja Prithviraj was taken prisoner and incarcerated in the fort of Hansi [Prithviraj was finally defeated in 1192]. This was followed by battles with [Gahadavala king] Raja Jai Chand, in which the legendary Adha and Udal were involved. The last and decisive battle was that of Orai in Bundelkhand, finally ending Hindu supremacy after great bloodletting. Thus the crown of Dehli passed on into the hands of the army of Islam. Therefore inscrutable are the ways of this transitory and undependable world of ours.

This poem dwells on the passing nature of this worldly life:

The cycle of springtide and autumnal fall/ gentle breeze and blowing wind/ sun and shade! Dried stubble and blooming fields! Music of rain and roar of thunder... glory of topless mansions of Dara and Sikandar, the fame of Behram, Nausherwan lying in the dust.

* The author has not given any sources for this chapter. The translator is unable to establish the historicity of the dates, the Maharajas that have been mentioned, and the period of their reigns.

A Brief Account of Muslim Monarchs

The Aryans hailed from the vast expanses of Central Asia and mass migrated to India by entering Punjab first. By brain and brawn, they soon occupied most of the northern parts of India, pushing the land's original inhabitants, the Dravidians, to the southern part of the vast country. Around the time of the advent of Islam, they had become so integrated into the land that they could be legitimately identified as the original inhabitants of the land called India. It is hard to ascertain why some Hindu kings chose the city of Dehli as their capital but later, the king of Dehli came to be recognized as the emperor or the 'king of kings'. In an informal sense, Dehli was acknowledged as the country's capital, and conquering Dehli symbolically meant the conquest of India. Hence the great importance of the city.

The Muslims turned their attention towards India for the first time during the reign of Hazrat Umar, the second caliph of Islam. However, these incursions were limited and mostly confined to the western parts of India, leaving Dehli almost untouched. Hence, it would be pretty tricky for a Dehli chronicler to mention them.

Arguably, the man who laid the foundation of Muslim rule in India was Mahmud Ghaznavi (or Ghazni). Ignited by ambition and religious fervour, like his father, Sabuktigin, Mahmud mounted as many as seventeen attacks on the Indian subcontinent, albeit confined to the north-western frontier and without touching Dehli. But call it greed or ambition, Mahmud later extended his forays into many other parts of the subcontinent: Kannauj in the north, Gwalior and Kalinjar in the central region, and Somnath in the southwest. As a result of the turmoil caused by Ghaznavi's invasions, the country did suffer, but Dehli remained safe.[1] The valour and ambitions of Mahmud were, however, not inherited by any of his successors. None could rule with a firm hand, resulting in a speedy deterioration. Then, the rising Ghoris began to overpower the weak Ghaznavis in Afghanistan, forcing them to flee to various parts of western India. This whetted the Ghoris' appetite.

Unusually, two Ghori brothers, Ghiyasuddin and Shihabuddin, had occupied the throne of Ghazni. Ghiyasuddin was the older and senior ruler, while Shihabuddin acted as his deputy. Practically, Ghiyasuddin was the administrator, and Shihabuddin, the commander-in-chief of the army, occupied the seat of power in the year 569 AH (1174). Shihabuddin was more ambitious. Like Mahmud (Ghaznavi), he too was bitten by the conquest bug. Once he had consolidated his rule in Afghanistan, after toiling for eleven years, in 580 AH (1184), he mounted an attack on Lahore. He forced the last of the Ghaznavid rulers, Khusrau Malik, into submission, compelling him to pay fiscal tribute, but he did not stop at that. Within three years, Khusrau Malik was thrown into prison, and Shihabuddin Ghori formally captured Lahore and Sialkot [both in present-day Pakistan].[2]

At that time, Prithviraj Chauhan, known as Rai Pithora, stood out as the ruler of the entire northern India. His capital was Ajmer not Dehli – where he had left his younger brother Khande Rao as vice-regent – was a pre-eminent part of his vast kingdom. Allegedly, he was more interested in enjoying a life of ease and comfort and had handed over the reins of governance to his chiefs and courtiers.[3] Khande Rao was known for his valour and equestrian skills. After several conquests, Shihabuddin Ghori turned his attention to Bhatinda [or Bathinda] in Punjab. After achieving success there, he decided to return to Ghazni, leaving some trusted chieftains in charge of state affairs in India. He had hardly finalized his departure date when information about Rai Pithora's advances came in. So he stayed on. A fierce battle soon took place at Thanesar[4] [in present-day Haryana], leading to direct combat between him and Khande Rao. Both suffered injuries, but the superior might of the Rajputs prevailed, resulting in the defeat of the Ghaznavid forces. However, this was not the final outcome. The soldiers of Islam were back to avenge their defeat the following year.

Khande Rao was killed in the battle [the Second Battle of Tarain]. Though Prithviraj fought valiantly, he was taken prisoner in the battlefield of Tarain on the banks of the Saraswati River.[5] Dehli and Ajmer were now taken by Ghori. Kannauj also fell within a year of Prithviraj's defeat, following which the rulers of Multan and other states accepted their defeat. The soldiers of Islam again proved their mettle in Bengal and Bihar, along with other adjoining areas:

Love puts one's own home above and better than the land of Suleiman
Even thorns are better than jasmine and basil
Though Yusuf ruled over the land of Egypt
Yet he put a beggar of Kanaan above his kingship.[6]

As the victorious Shihabuddin Ghori returned to Ghazni (Ghor), he appointed his favourite slave, Qutbuddin Aibak, as his vice-regent to rule over the newly conquered country. Qutbuddin proclaimed himself Sultan, with Dehli as his capital.[7] Thus, he became the first Muslim ruler of north India.[8]

List of Kings who Sat on the Throne of Dehli

Name of Family	Sl. No.	Name of the King	Year of accession	Year of death or dismissal	Remarks
Ghulaman Family	1	Qutubuddin Aibak	602 AH [1205]	607 AH [1210]	
	2	Aaram Shah	607 AH [1210]	607 AH [1210]	
	3	Sultan Shamsuddin Altamash	607 AH [1210]	633 AH [1235]	
	4	Sultana Razia	634 AH [1236]	637 AH [1239]	
	5	Moizuddin Behram Shah	637 AH [1239]	639 AH [1241]	
	6	Alauddin Masood	639 AH [1241]	644 AH [1246]	

	7	Naseeruddin Mahmood	644 AH [1246]	664 AH [1265]	
	8	Ghayasuddin Balban	664 AH [1265]	686 AH [1287]	
	9	Moizuddin Kaiqbad	686 AH [1287]	689 AH [1290]	
	10	Shamsuddin Kaikaous	689 AH [1290]	689 AH [1290]	

Khalji Family	1	Jalaluddin Khalji	689 AH [1290]	695 AH [1295]	
	2	Alauddin Khalji	695 AH [1295]	715 AH [1315]	
	3	Shahabuddin Bin Alauddin Khalji	715 AH [1395]	717 AH [1317]	
	4	Qutubuddin Mubarak Shah Bin Alauddin Khalji	717 AH [1317]	720 AH [1320]	
	5	Nasiruddin Khusroo Khan	720 AH [1320]	720 AH [1320]	

Tughlaqia Family	1	Ghayasuddin Tughlaq	720 AH [1320]	725 AH [1325]	
	2	Sultan Muhammad Adil	725 AH [1325]	752 AH [1351]	
	3	Sultan Firoz Shah	752 AH [1351]	790 AH [1388]	
	4	Sultan Tughlaq Shah	790 AH [1388]	791 AH [1389]	
	5	Abu Bakr Shah	791 AH [1389]	793 AH [1391]	
	6	Sultan Muhammad Shah	793 AH [1391]	796 AH [1393]	

	7	Alauddin Sikandar Shah	796 AH [1393]	796 AH [1393]	
	8	Sultan Mahmood Shah	796 AH [1393]	816 AH [1413]	

Saadat Family	1	Masnad Aali Syed Khizr Khan	816 AH [1413]	824 AH [1421]	
	2	Sultan Mubarak Shah	824 AH [1421]	837 AH [1433]	
	3	Sultan Muhammad Shah	837 AH [1433]	847 AH [1443]	
	4	Sultan Alauddin	847 AH [1443]	852 AH [1448] (Dismissal) 855 AH [1451] (Demise)	

Khalji Family	1	Bahlul Lodi	852 AH [1448]	894 AH [1489]	
	2	Sikandar Lodi	894 AH [1489]	914 AH [1508]	

Mughal Family	1	Shahabuddin Muhammad Shah Jahan Badshah	1048 AH [1638]	1068 (H) [1657] (Dismissal) 1076 (H) [1665] (demise)	Before that, Agra was declared the capital, which continued until the reign of Shah Jahan in 1048

	2	Emperor Alamgir (Aurangzeb)	1068 AH [1657]	1118 AH [1706]	
	3	Muhammad Moazzam Shah Alam Bahadur Shah Badshah	1118 AH [1706]	1124 AH [1712]	
	4	Muhammad Moizuddin Jahandar Shah Badshah	1124 AH [1712]	1125 AH [1713]	
	5	Azizuddin Muhammad Alamgir Sani Badshah	1167 AH [1753]	1172 AH [1758]	
	6	Abu Muzafar Shah Alam Badshah	1173 AH [1759]	1221 AH [1806]	
	7	Abu Nasr Moinuddin Akbar Shah Sani	1221 AH [1806]	1253 AH [1837]	
	8	Khatamusalateen Gorgani Hazrat Abu Zafar Sirajuddin Muhammad Bahadur Shah Sani	1253 AH [1837]	1277 AH (1857) (Dismissal) 1279 AH [1862] (Demise)	

Story of the Muslim Rule in India from 588 AH [1192] to 1273 AH [1759]

Historians record that in 588 AH [1192], Muizzuddin Sultan Shihabuddin Ghori [Muhammad Ghori], son of Bahauddin Shah of Ghazni,[1] (allegedly) launched as many as ten unsuccessful attacks on various territories of the Indian subcontinent. Only in his eleventh attempt[2] he succeeded in capturing the coveted throne, after which he issued a proclamation of kingship (*khutba*) and put his currency in circulation. He ruled for thirty-five years (in Ghor) and was followed by Qutbuddin Aibak (his subordinate in Dehli), who was both his slave and son-in-law.[3] Aibak ruled for only four years. After his demise came Aram Shah, who ruled for merely a year. Sultan Shamsuddin Altamash [Iltutmish], the revered one, succeeded him as the ruler of Dehli.

Sultan Altamash was a relative of Qutbuddin and also his son-in-law. He was a god-fearing man who strictly followed the Holy Book's tenets and the Prophet's traditions (PBUH). Altamash acquired the throne with the blessings of the great saint Khwaja Moinuddin Chishti. For his lawful living, he took to writing and stitching caps and always kept himself in a state of purity, following his ablutions and observing strict hygiene. Despite his kingly status, he believed in doing things on his own without the help of a retinue of servants. Even for post-midnight prayers (*tahajjud*), he did not seek anyone's help, for a bucket and rope were kept ready under his bedstead for drawing water. A man of high morals and a stickler for following the Sharia, he never spent state money on his personal needs, and this finds due mention in *Tzkaritul Arifeen*. He enrolled as a disciple of Khwaja Qutbuddin Bakhtiar Kaki and was conferred the authority of a vicegerent. He considered himself incredibly blessed and favoured to have given his preceptor the last bath after his demise. The Ghorid dynasty[4] ruled for 102 years and 27 days, with 11 rulers at the helm. Even today, many magnificent buildings stand as a reminder of the grand era.

In the scheme of the Creator, nothing lasts forever, and so after the Ghorids [actually Mamluks], the sun of the Khalji dynasty rose when one Shaista Khan, a scion of Turkic chief Khalji Khan, who was the son-in-law of Genghis Khan, rose to power. An army commander of Kaiqobad, he treacherously killed his master and declared himself the sultan, assuming the title of Sultan Jalaluddin Khalji. His dynasty produced four rulers, their rule lasting barely 34 years, 7 months and 20 days.

Sultan Qutbuddin Mubarak Shah was the last ruler of the Khalji dynasty. The cycle of treachery and betrayal was repeated when his favourite and trusted servant Hassan, who had newly embraced Islam, put him to death and usurped the throne of Dehli. He took the title of Khusrau Khan but met his end after ruling for just 4 months. He did not have any successor, so the fast-changing course of events ushered in the rise of the Tughlaq dynasty, beginning with Ghiyasuddin Tughlaq, a noble of the royal court.

The stately buildings constructed during the Tughlaq era stand as memorials to the dynasty – one that produced eight rulers, with their rule lasting for 96 years, 11 months and 19 days. There was then a watershed in the country's history after the death of Nasiruddin Mahmud, the last of the Tughlaqs.

This was the appearance of the great Amir Timur in India. He was, of course, our respected patriarch who conquered the city of Dehli. Yet he decided not to stay in Dehli and picked Malik Mardan to rule on his behalf. A Sayyid by birth and incomparable in valour and gallantry, Mardan ruled for some time but left no one to succeed him. Khan Maghri, the governor of Multan, receiving information, immediately left for Dehli. In league with other nobles and chiefs of the royal court, he issued a proclamation and got new currency minted and circulated in the name of Timur. Down the line, taking advantage of the void, he established his own rule and declared himself the legitimate ruler of the land. Three rulers from his family ruled over Dehli, and their rule lasted for merely 39 years, 7 months and 16 days. Sultan Alauddin Muhammad Shah was the last ruler, and his death paved the way for the rise of the Lodi dynasty.

Bahlol Lodi was the governor of the Sirhind region and bore the title of Khan-i-Khanan. Catching the weak powers (in Dehli) unawares before formally assuming the title of sultan, Bahlol first brought Punjab under his control. He proclaimed himself ruler in the year 808 AH and ruled for 38 years, 8 months and 7 days. He was succeeded by his son Sultan Sikandar Lodi, alias Prince Nizam Khan, who remained in power for 28 years and 5 months. After him came his son Sultan Ibrahim Lodi, who ruled for 7 years, when for some unknown reasons, one of his retainers, Madhu Shah Khatri, became ruler for some 5 months. However, the Madhushahi currency belonged to this brief period [Ibrahim Lodi, regained power]. The reign of the Lodis lasted for precisely 72 years, 6 months and 7 days. Sultan Ibrahim Lodi was the last ruler of this dynasty. He was killed in the First Battle of Panipat in the year 932 AH (1526) while fighting the invading forces of Sultan Zahiruddin Muhammad Babur.

Winning the battle, Babur made a triumphant entry into Dehli. As the [new] emperor, he conferred titles and honours on members of the nobility. He also directed Prince Humayun to proceed to Akbarabad [Agra] to take control of the situation. There, he came across Ibrahim Lodi's family, consisting of his mother, two sons and two wives. He took steps to provide them succour, earmarking Rs 7 lakh as an annual pension for their upkeep. He also arranged for Ibrahim Lodi's sons to be educated. Babur left for his heavenly abode five years and five months later. His son Nasiruddin Muhammad Humayun took his place, but fate did not fail to play its role as a spoiler. Within ten years, he faced the might of Sher Shah Suri, the rising Afghan chieftain of Bihar.

Sher Shah was the son of Farid Khan, the head of a small fiefdom, Sasaram. Courage and bravery rewarded him with successes in Odisha and Bengal, and he became a very effective ruler. At that point, a clash with Humayun became inevitable, and Sher Shah – after failing twice – succeeded in his third attempt to defeat Humayun, forcing him to leave

India. He proclaimed his kingship in the year 947 AH [1540] but only lived for five years after this event, though the reign of the Suris lasted for sixteen years and twenty-four days, with four kings in all – the last one being Sher Shah's nephew Adil Khan. The buildings constructed by this dynasty are still in existence.

The wheel then turned full circle as Humayun reconquered his lost territories in 962 AH [1555]. The Mughal dynasty, established by his father Babur, ruled for 498 years, producing 26 rulers.[5] The imposing buildings of this Gorgani-Timurid-Chagatai dynasty are all monuments of excellence and speak of the wealth of their builders. There is a strange coincidence concerning the life and death of the dynasty's first and last rulers, and thereby hangs a tale. While the patriarch, Amir Timur, was born on 28 Shabaan,[6] just before dawn, the unfortunate last king of the Gorgani dynasty, Bahadur Shah Zafar, was born on the same date, but after dusk. While one heralded the beginning of the great dynasty, the other represented the end of its glory. There are other similarities between the two as well. Timur had a son named Shahrukh Mirza, while the same was the name of one of the sons of Zafar – Mirza Shahrukh. That was not all. Both the patriarch and the last king's crown princes were also namesakes. Jalaluddin Miran Shah in the case of Timur and Mirza Dara Bakht Miran Shah, in the case of Bahadur Shah.

Tutī-Yi Hind[7] Ustad Zauq had admired him (the first heir-apparent and the author's father, Dara Bakht) in these words:

> O' royal one, you are as much a part of the lineage of your ancestor
> As one finds the Quran knit together with the Torah, Zabur, and Bible.[8]

During the reign of the last rulers, the emperor had no country left under his control. In addition, whatever land he still held, the British Resident was the virtual master of that. Yet, all proclamations were still issued in the emperor's name, the country was called his domain, and the minted currency bore his name. Besides, the traditional religious address in the mosques, on all Fridays, pronounced the name of the last Mughal emperor as the ruler of the time.

The treasury of the English East India Company had granted a monthly pension of Rs 1.35 lakh to Emperor Bahadur Shah, and, ostensibly, he was ceremoniously honoured as the Emperor of India. The English officers and even the governor received honours and titles from him. Even though the English were the real masters, the figurehead on the throne was the Mughal emperor. The country was practically governed by the English, and peace and tranquillity prevailed everywhere. The people were safe and at liberty to lead their lives free of worry. The ruling government was just, and the subjects were happy and content.

The Decline and Ruin of the City of Dehli[1]

Being the capital of a country is a matter of prestige and honour for a city – though it holds only when the government is stable, and the country is safe and secure. In such circumstances, prosperity prevails, and people enjoy all sorts of luxuries. But once things go awry and the glory of a regime declines, pride gives way to humiliation. The victorious turn on it to become the real masters. Everything that ever made sense becomes irrelevant. This is precisely what happened to the splendid city of Dehli. There was a general slump – socially, materially and in terms of moral values. Dehli was so beautiful, glorious and prosperous that its glory invited adversaries to come and eradicate it:

> Do not blame the flower and its picker, O' golden-throated nightingale!
> You have only to blame the sweetness of your song for your incarceration.[2]

Even a casual glance at the catastrophic occurrences in the city's history may bring tears to one's eyes. We do not have much idea about the Hindu period, but we know about the misfortunes that befell the city at different times during the Muslim period. Our great ancestor, Emperor Shah Jahan, declaring Dehli the seat of power of the Mughal Empire, revived its glory. Eminent nobles and princes made it their home, and a galaxy of intellectuals – men of letters and academics – made the capital into something that became the world's envy. It suffered some decline when Emperor Alamgir [Aurangzeb] turned his focus to his expeditions to the Deccan, but that was only a temporary phase. Once he was gone, another unfortunate period began with the struggle for succession.[3] Dehli, however, remained untouched by this conflict.

Later, Jahandar Shah's [r. 1712–13] efficiency turned his own family into his enemies. His nephew, Farrukh Siyar [r. 1713–19], succeeded in dethroning and imprisoning him – marking the beginning of the city's decline with the Syed [Syed brothers] and some other chiefs in the court also getting involved. Farrukh Siyar fell to the wrath of the two brothers, Syed Husain Ali Khan and Syed Abdullah Khan, whom he was planning to disempower. After that, the city, or even the once mighty Mughal Empire, could never regain its lost glory. Rulers like Rafiud Darajat [r. February–June 1719] and Rafiud Daulah [or Shah Jahan II, r. June–September 1719] occupied the throne for brief intervals, and that too only in name. They were not, in fact, kings but mere silhouettes.

The monarchy extinguished the lamps of many houses, but there was a limit to everything. There was such widespread disarray that the conspiring Saiyids, too, suffered from internecine rivalries. A wrong move by them resulted in Roshan Akhtar ascending the throne under the title of Muhammad Shah [r. 1719–48]. The Saiyid brothers had ignored Roshan Akhtar's wise and visionary mother, Qudsia Begum. Nobody seemed to have taken notice of her presence in the palace, nor was there anyone else fit for dispensing true governance. She, on her part, was well aware of her son's nature, temperament and capability. This made her wary.[4] The shrewd Saiyid brothers constantly posed problems. Somehow the king, on the advice of sincere and loyal courtiers, managed to post them apart in two far-off places to suppress the threat posed to the crown. This proved to be a relief for other nobles and powerful chiefs. Meanwhile, the scheme succeeded, and the clever brothers were finally eliminated.

Muhammad Shah, by disposition, was of a dissolute and lustful temperament. Often the provincial heads left their deputies at their headquarters and came over to Dehli to participate in their ruler's endless merrymaking and revelries.[5] A deceptive calm prevailed for some time but not for long as the covetous Nadir Shah, the ruler of Persia and Afghanistan, was keeping an eye out for an opportunity to launch an attack on Dehli and seize the riches of the Indian subcontinent. On the pretext of the murder of his envoy to the Mughal court, he entered the country from Punjab and attacked Dehli. Muhammad Shah responded leisurely, despatching his debauched henchmen and favourite courtiers to halt the enemy's advances. The outcome was evident and he had only himself to blame for the subsequent carnage that claimed hundreds and thousands of lives. This dealt an irrevocable blow to Dehli, and Nadir Shah returned, having stripped the city of all its wealth and glory. It took a long time for its economy and opulence to recover and for the wounds to heal. After Nadir Shah's death, his military commander and successor (in Afghanistan), Ahmed Khan Durrani, took his chance invading the Indian subcontinent.[6] However, this time, Prince Ahmed Shah, along with the wise minister Qamruddin led a counter-attack and, after a brief encounter, forced the enemy to take to his heels and retreat. This incidentally was fated to be the last victory of the Mughals, and a tale of repeated defeats and humiliations played out after this.

At this juncture, the provincial chiefs, recognizing an opportunity in the weakness of the centre, took to the path of secession, resulting in a free-for-all. This situation also resulted in the rise of Maratha supremacy and the gradual eclipse of the Mughal Empire. However, 1761 brought about the defeat of the vast Maratha army at the hands of Ahmed Shah Abdali in the Third Battle of Panipat. This defeat resulted in the large-scale killing of the Maratha chiefs and soldiers, but the mischievous Marathas still did not abstain from looting and rampage in Dehli. Even the silver-plated ceiling of Diwan-i-Aam was pulled out, and the heavy string of pearls which the Mughal queens, princesses and begums had hung in Moti Masjid was looted.

In the meantime, Shah Alam II [first r. 1760–88] had returned to claim the throne.[7] But the worst was yet to come. Ghulam Qadir Rohilla, once a favourite of Shah Alam II, rose to power in the palace. He virtually ruled inside the fort, resorting to all sorts of atrocities. In 1789, he gouged out Emperor Shah Alam II's eyes in a bloody act of vendetta, letting loose a wave of vandalism and looting in the fort.[8] Later, Maratha chief Mahadeoji Scindia[9] avenged the emperor's dishonour at the hands of the Rohillas and eliminated Ghulam Qadir from the scene. Still, by then, Dehli had already been divested of much of its charm and grandeur.

Emperor Shah Alam wrote of his plight in a poignant Persian poem*, the original of which I could not find; a translation is as follows:

> Tragedy and calamity after calamity took away all the charm and grandeur of my empire, leaving it barren and deserted. The glorious sun was eclipsed, caving into the final darkness. I feel lucky to have become blind, for, at least this way, I do not have to see the devastation with my own eyes. All this is reminiscent of the evil army of cursed Yazid at Karbala. In this case, my unfaithful servants let loose all sorts of atrocities on me. My worldly wealth was like an ailment, tormenting me. Now, as I am stripped of it, I have recovered from my illness by the grace of the Almighty, and at the same time, I have been chastised for my sins and faults. I feel the Almighty has forgiven all my sins!
>
> Alas! I crushed snakes but reared their young ones. Indeed, I am responsible for my downfall. Those swearing their loyalty to me finally betrayed me; all my nobles deserted me at the critical moment; all my savings in three decades have gone! Manzoor Ali Khan stood by

me, but he was helpless. Both the Mughal and Pathan chiefs and courtiers conspired to finish me. Hamadan's ambassador and notorious Ghul Muhammad, Allah Yaar Suleman, and Badal Beg all united and aimed at eradicating me. On top of it all, joining hands in this venture, the Afghan youth [Ghulam Qadir] snuffed the light of the empire itself. O All-Wise and All-Seeing, now I am a blind man who cannot see anything except Your Divine Light.

The brave Timur Shah,[10] however, came to my rescue. Of course, Mahadeoji Scindia, like my son, also came over to rescue me. I wish my loyal servant Asafuddaulah and the English officers to join hands, rid me of my predicament, and take revenge for my humiliations. I desire the princes and all the subjects to join hands in making me secure.

Of all the Queens, only Mubarak Mahal remains with me.

But 'Aftab',[11] be patient; time does not always stay the same. Now my only hope is God Almighty.[12]

What a poignant and disturbing piece! How revolting! After that, the real power shifted to Mahadeoji Scindia, and his writ ran throughout the palace and the city. The emperor had virtually delegated his powers to the Marathas after becoming sightless, and the whole country practically came under the control of the Marathas: tragedy after tragedy! But how long could that last too? Finally, Lord Lake, the British General, captured Dehli in 1802.[13] He rescued the emperor from the clutches of the Marathas and allowed him to retain the titular monarchy of the Indian subcontinent. The English also sanctioned a monthly pension of Rs 1.25 lakh** for royal expenses. At least ostensibly, the emperor's control over the fort remained undisturbed – the conferring of honours and titles continued to be his prerogative; the royal currency remained a legal tender in the provinces as well; and, of course, gifts and tributes continued to pour in from all over. This is not to deny that this was an unrealistic situation, but at least it provided a veneer, which somehow continued till the eruption of the revolt of 1857. The revolt was the event that drove the final nail in the coffin of the Mughal Empire and Dehli, its capital. There is now no real Dehli. Of course, the city is there, but the dwellers who made it Dehli are nowhere to be seen:

> O Talib, Dehli resembles a lifeless body,
> Those who were indeed the soul of Dehli have passed away.[14]

Here (for the record), we offer the text of the contract signed (before the Company's takeover of Dehli) by the

Mughal emperor [Shah Alam II], ceding the *Diwani* [the right to collect taxes on behalf of the emperor] of Bengal and Bihar [and Odisha] to the East India Company for just Rs 26 lakh per annum. It has been sourced from a book of history in English. It goes as follows:

> High on devotion and loyalty, a faithful servant in deed and spirit exemplifies noble actions.... In acknowledgement of the Company's noble services, we very gladly and with extreme willingness have decided that the *Diwani* of Bengal, Bihar, and Odisha [with effect from 1765] ... is being handed over to and bestowed upon the East India Company in totality. In our capacity and by dint of the power entrusted to us, we have further decided to exempt them from paying the annual tributary amount. In lieu of that, the grantee would be obliged to pay a yearly amount of rupees twenty-six lakh, previously paid by the Nawab Nazim [Governor] of Bengal. The same responsibility would hereby pass on to the Company. As per our pleasure, this order takes effect from the eighth day of the month of Safar ul Muzaffar[15] in the sixth year of our coronation.[16]

This instrument of settlement, in effect, made the Company the actual master of Bengal province. The Company dismissed the Nawab Nazim, the administrator of

Bengal, on account of his irregularities, and appointed its governor.

Later, following the conquest of Dehli, the Governor-General mooted a proposal for fixing the pension of Emperor Shah Alam II, along with his expenses. The proposal was approved with a few amendments. The following is the translation of the correspondence by Lord Wellesley (the then governor-general) on the subject:

> From the Governor-General-in-Council to the members of the Court of Directors,
> Fort William, Calcutta, 2 June 1805.
>
> May it please Your Excellencies.
>
> The Governor-General-in-Council requests to submit the following arrangement to sanction the amount for the expenses of Emperor Shah Alam II and the members of the royal family. The rationale of the same would be explained herein:
>
> There is, of course, no intention whatsoever on this government's part to fix the pension, in a design to impinge on his existing powers or to meddle with them in any way, on the pretext of providing him with due security and safeguards, against the ongoing manoeuvrings of his enemies. Our intentions are clear and honest, and thus, there is no question of any attempt on our part to gain

control over any area under the Mughal empire or any of the provincial dominions attached to it; nor can we ever entertain the thought of making the provincial chiefs and feudal landlords [sic] less respectful towards His Majesty, the emperor, in any way. Of course, the governor-general wishes to get some benefits in return for the arrangements made for His Majesty's safety, security and well-being, which have been explained in our letter, dated 13th July [of the previous year].

The Governor-General is highly keen to safeguard all the interests of the emperor and his family members, as has been our endeavour. On the other hand are the machinations of the Marathas in general and the motives of the French in particular, to undermine the British authority, in whatever way may be possible, by drawing a wedge and creating misunderstandings between His Majesty and us. In this connection, we draw your kind attention to the communication [Paragraph 73], which provides ample proof of the French design, to take over the custody of Shah Alam II into their hands at the cost of the cordial relations existing between the British and His Majesty. When the Company is firmly in the saddle in Dehli, all such machinations have fallen flat.

The Governor-General-in-Council has been particularly troubled by the attempts of the Marathas and the French. He fully appreciates the stress upon and hardships of the emperor in this advanced age of his, and so they [sic] cannot surely turn a blind eye to his plight. Hence, the anxiety on the part of the Governor-General is to ensure His Majesty the much-needed peace and equanimity at this stage. After taking over the reins of governance, the British have paid particular attention to this facet and have worked out a good financial package in keeping with His Majesty's dignity, honour and status – aptly so in the context of their traditional mutual interests. The safety and security of His Majesty and his family members is a matter of highest priority for us. The governor-general has therefore worked out a scheme of pension and salary for him.

The Governor-General-in-Council, thereby, is of the view that the entire area, along the banks of the Yamuna, would remain under the control of the royal family. For that purpose, these lands would be placed under the power of the Resident of Dehli. The revenue would be collected and dispersed justly for the benefit of the royal family.

By the rules and regulations formed by the Company, the emperor would be entitled to appoint a *Diwan* [superintendent], along with a few functionaries, to keep a vigil on all affairs. They would be positioned in the collector's office and keep the emperor updated with all developments to his satisfaction. This way, due control over the accounts may also be ensured. The courts would continue to dispense justice following the Sharia law. Still, cases involving long-term punishment or the death penalty would invariably be referred to His Majesty for final approval.

In addition to the lands allotted to His Majesty, with a noble intention to compensate for his needs and requirements, the following scheme of payment of pension and grants per month has been approved:

The Scheme of Payments

His Majesty: Rs 80,000
Heir-Apparent (Land Apart): Rs 10,000
Prince Mirza Izzat Baksh – son of His Majesty: Rs 5,000
For two minor sons of His Majesty: Rs 1,500 and Rs 3,000
For fifty young children of His Highness, in total: Rs 10,000
Shah Nawaz Khan – the Royal Treasurer: Rs 2,500
Syed Raza Khan – Agent of the government, attached to His Majesty: Rs 1,000

Total: Rs 1,11,500

If the lands allotted to His Majesty fail to fulfil the royal expenses, the monthly remuneration may be raised to Rs

1 lakh. In addition to the above-recorded amounts, a sum of Rs 10,000 per annum would be paid to His Majesty to celebrate various festivals, etc.

Signature
Wellesley, Barlow, Edney [17]

[Translator: After the demise of Shah Alam II, his son Akbar Shah II occupied the throne under identical conditions imposed by the English. Bahadur Shah Zafar followed him, the last Mughal figurehead.]

The Company's top brass accepted almost all the grants recorded above. The emperor's pension was raised to Rs 1 lakh per month, following an increment of Rs 20,000. In addition, an amount of Rs 10,000 was also granted for the maintenance and repair of the fort and other buildings. In that miserable condition, Dehli had somehow attained some stability, at least for the time being.

Suddenly, in 1273 AH [1857], some imprudent soldiers raised the issue of the cartridges,[18] and, resultantly, the mutiny took place. A few army units at the Meerut Cantonment revolted. Overpowering and murdering their English officers, they subsequently marched to Dehli. The royal guards posted at the gates of the grand wall of the city, quite injudiciously, opened the doors, and the rebel army swooped in. Then, the army stationed at Dehli cantonment, not being worth their salt, also joined them. All possible terrors and tyrannies were let loose on the city. A proclamation was made in the capital that all men were the creation of the Almighty, the country belonged to the emperor, and that the soldiers' writ was in force in the city. Some of the rebels and their officers were no less than barbarians. They openly said, 'Brother, we can put the crown on anybody's head, and he would become the king.' Some even proclaimed, 'Get rid of everything, shoot the old man [the emperor] and make any other person the king.'

The hapless emperor was thus at the mercy of the agitators. They controlled all his actions and movements. As the emperor was 84 years old, he was powerless to get rid of them. Indeed, it was not a rebel army but a calamity, like an angel of death. The outcome was that the rebels lived a life of luxury and comfort in the grand dwelling of the capital for four and a half months during the rainy season. They fought with their masters [the English] and later fled the city. Hence, the ultimate victims were none other than the city and the populace of Shahjahanabad [Dehli]. Thousands lost their lives. The mischievous soldiers settled their scores on the pretext of the revolt. The royal family was crushed and smashed forever. The ordinary people were hurled out of their city, and many were eliminated. The looters' writ prevailed. Nobody was there to come to the rescue of the affected. The truth is that nobody could do anything as it was the wrath of the Almighty against a nation; who could save them? The British authorities showed exemplary generosity and open-heartedness at that deadly moment of hunger and want. God will give them compensation for the noble act. In keeping with the holy spirit, they granted each of the afflicted a stipend of five rupees per month.

Such examples were many. The British did not flinch when Shah Shuja, the ruler of Kabul, being victimized by his minister, Dost Muhammad Khan, sought protection. They offered all help to the members of the Afghan royal family. They spent lakhs of rupees on the Afghan king, virtually nourished him, and appointed many of his kin to high positions. Similarly, the British government granted a pension of Rs 2,000 per month in perpetuity to the family members of Prince Mirza Ilahi Baksh. They were also compensated with lakhs of rupees for their losses. Their property was protected, and all the customary concessions remained intact. The late Ilahi Baksh's family still enjoys all the rewards.[19]

Additionally, after the fall of Kashgar, the British allocated a monthly stipend of Rs 850 to the envoy who was posted there. This is not all, as shown by the case of Prince Firoze Shah, who had joined the rebel forces and fought against the government in various places. He later strayed into the wilderness of Bukhara, Iran, Russia, Rome, etc. After he died in Mecca, the British granted his widow a pension of Rs 100 per month from the Bombay treasury. Similar was the experience of the provincial governors and princes, be it the Maharajas of Patiala, Jind and Nabha, or even the Begum of Bhopal. Some other governors and local lords were allocated fiefdoms. Further, Amir Ayub Khan – a great rebel – also found refuge under the British after all his peregrinations. The government granted him a pension of Rs 20,000 per month.

The case of Maharaja Dalip Singh was no different. He, too, had gone against the English but returned to their fold after finding all other avenues closed to him. The government patronized him and gave various positions to his children. During the tenure of His Honour Nawab Sir James Loyal, pensions of Rs 250 per month were also granted to the elder members of the Mughal royal family and even to the widowed women in the family, on the recommendation of Mr R. Clark.[20]As a result, the royal family has a general impression that the government has felt pity for us because it has tested our loyalty during the last thirty-seven years (after the revolt of 1857). Therefore, we believe that the British government will keep patronizing us.

I have no hesitation in saying that India has been fortunate to have a government full of compassion and restraint. This state of affairs places an outstanding obligation on us to follow the commands of our rulers and pledge our loyalty to them. It is our privilege that our rulers are so considerate towards us. It is a universal principle that the people in power and their subjects can never enjoy equal status. Hence, we should never expect such equality. However, our [British] authorities are of such nature that they shower kindness and honour on all those [Indians] who visit them [for whatever purpose]. When even this humble self happens to meet the British authorities, they bestow such kindness and sympathy upon this poor and worthless soul that it is exemplary. We should feel content with whatever is in our hands, as even that is sufficient.

* Shah Alam was an accomplished poet writing in Persian, Urdu, Braj. His *takhallus* was Aftab. He produced 4 Urdu Diwans, which are lost, and one Persian called the *Diwan-i Aftab*. A volume of his work exists entitled *Nadirat-i Shahi* containing verses in Urdu, Braj and Persian. He is also said to have authored a Dastan.

** For more details on the provenance, amount and reasons for the pension issue, see: Amar Farooqui, *Zafar and the Raj*

An Account of Existing Monuments in Shahjahanabad, Dehli

No.	Monument Name	Year of construction	Description
1	JAMA MASJID	1066 AH [1655]	This mosque was built in the period and under the care of Shah Jahan Badshah, Saadullah Khan, and Afzal Khan. In addition to stones, porterage, and other equipment, it was built with the expense of Rs 10 lakh and completed in six years, where more than five thousand masons and daily wagers worked on it daily. Its foundation stone, laid on 10 Shawwal [Arabic Month] 1060 AH, was 60 yards in length and 30 yards in width. Around it, there was a red sandstone bowl. Emperor Alamgir [Aurangzeb] built courtyards around it.

2	MASJID FATEHPURI		This mosque, too, was built in the period of King Shah Jahan Badshah by his second wife.
3	ZEENATUL MASAJID	1112 AH [1700]	This mosque is named after Nawab Zeenatun Nisa Begam Sahiba, daughter of King Shah Jahan Badshah. Her shrine is also located there in Dariya Ganj.
4	MASJID DAREEBA KALAAN	1115 AH [1703]	Built by Nawab Sharfuddaula.
5	SUNEHRI [GOLDEN] MASJID	1134 AH [1721]	This mosque is adjacent to Kotwali [police station]. Nawab Roshanuddola built it.
6	FAKHRUL MASAJID	1141 AH [1728]	This mosque is near Kashmiri Gate.
7	SECOND SUNEHRI MASJID	.	This mosque is under the Fort, towards Faiz Bazaar and Dariya Ganj.
8	KAALI MASJID		This mosque was built by King Firoze Shah.
9	DARGAH HAZRAT SHAH TURKMAN BAYABANI	958 AH [1551]	Accounts of him can be well obtained from historical books on Sufism.
10	DARGAH HAZRAT SYED FATEH ALI SHAH QADRI		Named after the king His Highness Hazrat Gohar Shah Aalam.
11	OLD GIRJAGHAR [CHURCH]	1266 AH [1849]	Colonel Oscar built it at the cost of Rs 90,000.
12	JAIN MANDIR [DHARAMPURA]		It was built at the cost of Rs 5 lakh.

13	MALKA BAGH MEANS GARDEN OF HER MAJESTY THE QUEEN	1060 AH [1650]	This garden belongs to Jahan Aara Begam Sahiba, daughter of King Shah Jahan. After the Ghadar [mutiny], it was expanded further. Now it is famous as Malka Ka Bagh [Garden of Queen]. There is a gorgeous villa situated within it.
14	GHANTA GHAR	.	This was built after the Ghadar [mutiny].
15	MADRASA NAWAB NIZAM DAKAN [SOUTH]	.	It is located in front of Ajmeri Gate. Now there is a school named Nawab Fund there.
16	SALEEM GARH	958 AH [1551]	Built in the period of King Shah Saleem.
17	NEELI CHHATRI	.	This was the fishing ground of King Shah Saleem in Saleem Garh.
18	BAGH [GARDEN] ROSHAN AARA	.	Roshan Ara was the daughter of King Aurangzeb Alamgir.[1] She built the garden. Apart from being an author, she was also a calligrapher.
19	BAGH MAHALDAAR KHAN	1140 AH [1727]	It was built in the period of King Mohammad Shah and was situated in Sabzi Mandi. The market has since been destroyed.
20	BAGH-E-QUDSIYAH		It belonged to Nawab Qudsiyah Begam Saheba and was built after King Mohammad Shah. It is situated outside Kashmiri Gate.
21	KOTHI THOMAS METCALFE SAHAB		It was built in the period of King Hazrat Abu Zafar Sirajuddin Bahadur Shah. Metcalfe was given the title of Farzande [son] Arjumand by the King, land worth Rs 12,000, and some cash from the Royal Treasury.

22	QILA MU'ALLA (RED FORT)	1058 AH [1648]	The construction of this fort began during King Shah Jahan's reign. It contains the following buildings: • Chhatta Lahori • Darwaza [Lahori Gate] • Naqqar Khana • Deewan-e-Aam [Hall of Audience] • Deewan-e-Khaas [Hall of Special Audience] • Meezan ka Daalan [Courtyard of Meezan] • Baithak [Meeting Hall] • Khuab Gah [Bedroom] • Tasbeeh Khana [Chanting Room] • Burj-e-Shama Maa Jharoka [Tower of light with window] • Rang Mahal • Asad Burj [Tower] behind the bathroom • Dalaan [Courtyard] Jajah Khana • Moti Masjid [Mosque] Alamgiri • Zafar Mahal [Zafar Palace]. This Baradari [square building or pavilion with twelve doors designed to allow the free flow of air] was built by King Abu Zafar Bahadur in 1258 AH. • Jal Mahal [Water Palace]. This was built of red sandstone in Mehtab Bagh [Mehtab Garden] by King Abu Zafar in 1253 AH. Its king tower has been removed. Details of the destroyed buildings in RED FORT: • Taup Khana [Artillery], Mehtab Bagh, Hayat Bakhsh Bagh [Life-saving garden], Chaubeen Mosque, Khan Samani, Bawarchi khana [Kitchen]

			• Sawan Bhado [named on the two months of the Hindu calendar] Now there are courtyards for all of them, courtyards of Ghulam Gardish, Deewane Khas for both front rooms, Astabal Khas [notable stables], Courtyards of Deewane Aam, Gulal Bar [a wall which prevents entrance or passage through it]. It was in front of Deewan-i Aam and built of red sandstone in reticulated shape and equal in height to a man, Down Gatehouse, Chhoti Baithak Mahal [Palace for minor assembly], Wali-e Ahad Mahal Saraye [Palace Inn for Crown Prince], Aish Mahal [Palace for enjoyment], new mohalla [new neighbourhood], two markets and other mosques, Darya Mahal [River Palace], Rang Mahal [Colour Palace] and other special palaces for Sahibzadas [sons of kings] and Bawan Chowk [fifty-two squares] which were meant for accommodation of female professional students.
23	DARGAH [SHRINE] OF HAZRAT KHUAJA QUTUBUDDIN BAKHTIYAR KAKI	948 AH [1541]	King Farrukh Sair fixed marble lattices at the shrine and built the Gate of Aastanah.
24	MOSQUE AND DARGAH KHUAJAH SAHAB	1120 AH [1708]	This mosque is older, and the year given is for the renovation of the mosque.
25	DARWAZAH MAHAL SHAHI [GATE OF ROYAL PALACE] IN QUTUB		All palaces are in ruins. However, this gate remains. King Hazrat Abu Zafar built it.

26	MOTI MASJID [MOTI MOSQUE]	1121 AH [1709]	This mosque behind the Dargah of Khuajah Saheb, built of marble, still exists. It has a tomb of marble. In this dargah, there are other shrines, such as Shah Alam Bahadur, His Highness, Gohar Shah Aalam Akbare Saani [second Akba], Mirza Fathul Mulk [third son of Abu Bakar Bahadur Shah]. In the compound of the dargah, there are many tombs of the princes of the Timur family.
27	QILA RAI PITHORA [PITHORA FORT]	1198 AH [1783]	Rai Pithora built it in the Vikramaditya era, and its ruins still exist.
28	MASJID QUWWATUL ISLAM	592 AH [1196]	Sultan Shamsuddin Altamash built this mosque in place of a temple built by Raja Prithviraj, but it remained incomplete.
29	QUTUB MINAR	616 AH [1219]	This is a minaret of Masjid Quwwatul Islam. The second minaret is incomplete.
30	TOMB OF UDHAM KHAN	969 AH [1561]	It was built in the period of Akbar the Great. Udham was the milk brother of Akbar.
31	KOTHI THOMAS SAHAB, RESIDENT OF DEHLI	------	It was built in the period of King Abu Zafar. Before that, it was the tomb of Udham Khan's brother. The dome still exists.
32	JHARNAH [WATERFALL] QUTUB SAHAB	1143 AH [1730]	-----------
33	DARGAH SULTAN GHAZI SAHAB	------	Situated on the western side of Dargah Qutub Sahab, this shrine is two miles from Qutub Sahab.
34	JOG MAYA TEMPLE	1233 AH [1817]	This place is old and excellently constructed in the documented year.
35	MINARE AAHINI [IRON PILLAR]	1198 AH [1783]	It was fixed in 1198 AH, according to mantra shastra. Later, the king had it installed in the yard of his mosque.

36	DARGAH IMAM ZAMIN	1044 AH [1634]	Dargah of a great Sufi.
37	DARGAH MAULANA JAMALI SAHAB	935 AH [1528]	It exists near Aastanah of Khuajah and between Kothi Thomas and the Garden of Nazir.
38	DARGAH BIWI [WIFE] NOOR		It is said that this shrine falls on the way to Qutub Sahab. Biwi Noor was Rabia Basri [a world-renowned Arab Sunni Muslim saint and Sufi mystic] of her time.
39	SAFDAR JUNG TOMB	1060 AH [1650]	It is three miles from Shahjahanabad and was built by Nawab Shujauddaulah.
40	JANTAR MANTAR	1137 AH [1724]	Built by Raja Jai Singh, the monarch of Jaipur.
41	DARGAH [SHRINE] HAZRAT SULTAN NIZAMUDDIN AULIYA	--	It was built over a prolonged period, during the reigns of several kings.
42	MASJID SULTAN JI	710 AH [1310]	There is a golden bowl in this mosque which Firoze Shah offered. It hangs with the help of a 14-yard-long chain.
43	DARGAH [SHRINE] AMEER KHUSROO	1014 AH [1605]	This shrine is in Astanah Sultan Ji. There are many other caliphs of Sultan Ji in this shrine.
44	TOMB OF JAHAN ARA BEGAM	1054 AH [1644]	She was the daughter of Shah Jahan. It is on the lower side of the Sultan Ji Shrine.
45	TOMB OF PRINCE MIRZA JAHANGEER	_	It was built in the period of Akbar II. The courtyard is slightly higher than the shrine.
46	CHOSAT KHAMBA [64 PILLARS]	_	This monument was built of marble in the period of Akbar the Great.
47	DOME OF TIKKA KHAN	_	This dome belongs to the foster father of Akbar the Great, located in Dargah Sultan Ji.

48	DARGAH MAKHDOOM NASEERUDDIN CHARAGH DEHLI	775 AH [1373]	King Firoze Shah built this in the courtyard of the shrine. Built of marble, it also contains the shrine of this author's father.
49	TOMB OF SIKANDAR LODI	775 AH [1373]	This shrine is situated in the Dargah of Makhdoom Naseeruddin.
50	DARGAH SHEIKH SALAHUDDIN	752 AH [1351]	Near Dargah Makhdoom Sahab.
51	QILA TUGHLAQ [TUGHLAQ FORT]	–	
52	TOMB OF TUGHLAQ	726 AH [1326]	Adjacent to Tughlaqabad.
53	MASJID KHIDKI	789 AH [1387]	Now, it is surrounded by a village, but the mosque is abandoned.
54	MASJID MOTH	909 AH [1503]	There are many stories relating to this mosque.
55	KALKA MANDIR	1178 AH [1764]	In the past, there was a Baradari here. Rai Kedarnath built the temple in 1231 AH.[2]
56	BARAHPULA (12 PIERS)	1021 AH [1612]	It was constructed in the period of King Jahangir.
57	DARAGAH SYED MAHMOOD BAHAR	778 AH [1376]	This is located near Barahpula [12 piers]. He was a great Muslim Sufi.
58	HUMAYUN TOMB		It was built in the period of Akbar the Great. A king is resting under the courtyard of this tomb. The tomb of Dara Shikoh is also situated there.
59	KARAM KHURDA BUNGALOW	1192 AH [1778]	It was built in the period of His Highness King Gohar Shah Alam.
60	SHER MANDAL [SHER SHAH'S PAVALLION]	950 AH [1543]	Built by King Sher Shah.
61	TOMB OF KHAN KHANA		Built in the period of Akbar the Great.

62	JAIL KHANA DEHLI [PRISON]	.	In the past, this was a travellers' house. After that, the Government of India, in a systematic way, constructed a prison there.
63	DARGAH QADAM SHAREEF	776 AH [1374]	
64	DARGAH BAQI BILLAH	1012 AH [1603]	This great Sufi saint was the originator and pioneer of the Naqshbandi order in the Indian subcontinent and had a significant following in India.
65	DARGAH DEEN ALI SHAH	_	This is the shrine of the great Sufi Saint Majzoob [Majzoob refers to that state of being immersed in the inner plane and divorced from the outside world] from the period of Abu Zafar Shah. This is near Dargah Hazrat Baqi Billah.
66	DARGAH SYED HUSN-E-RASOOL NUMA	778 AH [1376]	He was a very famous Dervish.
67	KOTLA FIROZ SHAH	775 AH [1373]	There is a pillar made of granite very close to the city.
68	FATEHGARH	_	Built after the Ghadar... It was under the control of European forces at that time.
69	QASR-i SAFED [WHITE PALACE]	599 AH [1202]	King Qutubuddin Ghori built it. Now there is no sign of it.[3]
70	QILA LA'AL Yaani KAUSHAK LAL [T]	71 AH [690]	Sultan Ghayasuddin Balban built it. There are some remaining traces of the fort in Ghayaspur.
71	QILA HAZAAR SUTOON [FORT OF THOUSAND COLUMNS]	90 AH [708]	Sultan Jalaluddin Khalji built it. Now there are no signs of the fort.[4]
72	SHAH BAGH [ROYAL GARDEN]	1294 AH [1877]	King Abu Zafar Bahadur Shah built it near Shahdara.

73	MASJID ISA KHAN	984 AH [1576]	It was built in the period of Sultan Islam Shah.
74	ARAB SARAI	958 AH [1551]	This was built in the period of Emperor Humayun. There are many unique monuments inside it.
75	BURJ FARHAT IFTARA [SABZ BURJ]	1131 AH [1718]	This tower is within the Humayun's Tomb monument.[5]
76	TOMB OF GHAYASUDDIN	882 AH [1477]	It is located in Mehrauli.
77	OKHLA BARRAGE	_	It was built after the Ghadar [treason], on the order of highest authority, and is a spectacular monument.
78	QILA KOHNA OR PURANA QILA [OLD FORT]	_	It is famous as Purana Qila. First, it was built by the Pandavas, and then it collapsed. In 733 AH, King Nekpal rebuilt it; then Emperor Humayun renovated it. A mosque was also built by Akbar the Great inside it.
79	Haft Manzil [Seven Storeys]		This palace, under Purana Qila, was built by Emperor Humayun. Its ruins still exist.

The British at the Helm of India

Sir Thomas Roe arrived in the court of Emperor Akbar[1] as the envoy of the British monarch[2] in 1215 AH [1800]. The emperor received him with due honour. The credit for opening trade relations with India indeed goes to the efforts of Sir Thomas. During Emperor Jahangir's reign, the East India Company opened its offices at different centres in Surat, Ahmedabad, Madras, and Calcutta. The opening of such trade operations began to yield positive results to the advantage of India.[3] This led to several concessions for the Company, so much so that the Mughal court decided to forego taxes in 1616.[4]

Notably, from 1616 to 1772, the Company fought several battles[5] with local forces and always emerged victorious. Warren Hastings was appointed to the post of governor-general in 1774.[6] The first thing he did was to move the headquarters of the Bengal Presidency from Murshidabad to Calcutta. He instituted civil courts and high [*sadar*] boards. During his tenure, the ruler of Banaras revolted, clashes with the Rohillas happened, and the Mysore War[7] took place. The unrest among the begums of Awadh followed.

Lord Cornwallis succeeded Warren Hastings as the governor-general in 1785,[8] and he introduced the scheme of Permanent Settlement. He appointed thousands of nawabs and rajas and gave increments to the employees of the Company. The Third Anglo-Mysore War took place in 1789,[9] and under a new law enacted in 1793, proprietary rights to land were granted to the landlords. Cornwallis was awarded the title of Marquess for his exceptional contributions. Sir John Shore followed him as governor-general towards the end of 1793. Conflicts arose between the Marathas and Tipu Sultan during his tenure. After him came the Marquess of Wellesley [term of office: 1798–1805], during whose tenure the Marathas were subjugated after the Second Maratha War [1803–05]. The region of Karnataka and the province of Odisha were annexed to the territory of the East India Company. Mysore was conquered after the Fourth Anglo-Mysore War [1798 –99]. Lord Wellesley was made a Duke.

Lord Cornwallis came in for a second term in India after him, but he died within a few months of his arrival. A war with the Marathas was fought during this period.

After that, Lord Sir George Barlow became the governor-general in 1807,[10] and under him, a pact was signed with the Holkars. A Sepoy Revolt occurred in Madras Presidency. After him, Lord Minto became the governor-general in 1813.[11] He signed peace treaties with Maharaja Ranjit Singh[12] and many other local rulers during his tenure. Kabul and Iran also signed pacts with the Company. After him, Lord Hastings [1813–23] took over as governor-general again* and ordered a military expedition against Nepal in 1814. After several encounters, the ruler of Nepal negotiated for peace and ceded several forts to the Company in the regions of Kumaon, Garhwal and Terai. During his tenure, the Pindaris were uprooted and the state of Gwalior was subjugated. Subsequently, peace prevailed, and Hastings left for home in 1823. He was succeeded by Lord Amherst [1823–28]. During his time, Bharatpur was vanquished, the ruler of Burma was knocked off his pedestal,[13] and the demarcation of the borders up to Ceylon was made.

After Amherst's return to England in 1828, William Bailey officiated for some time till Lord William Bentinck [1828–35] arrived as the new governor-general. This period has become known for the vital administrative and social reforms Bentinck undertook. The ruler of Coorg [in present-day Karnataka] ceded his territory to the Company; the thugs were uprooted; the custom of Sati and the practice of human sacrifice made before the idol of Kali were put to an end. Lord Bentinck met with an unfortunate accident necessitating his return to England. For some time, Sir Charles Metcalfe [1835–36] officiated on his behalf. A law for the freedom of the press was passed during his tenure.

In 1836, Lord Auckland [1836–42] became the governor-general. His tenure was marked by war with China in 1843, resulting in Hong Kong surrendering to the British. The war with Kabul saw Dost Mohammad Khan being taken prisoner and brought to India. In the same year, 1842, Lord Ellenborough [1842–44] took over as governor-general, and during his tenure, Kabul was conquered. The region of Sind also came under British occupation, and a war with Gwalior took place.[14] Lord Dalhousie [1848–56] took over as governor-general in 1848. During his time, Punjab was annexed, and a treaty was signed with Maharaja Dalip Singh; the Second Anglo-Burmese War took place, in which the Company gained considerably; and the territory of Nagpur was also annexed. During the same period, the telegraph system and railways were introduced in India. In 1856, Lord Canning [1856–57, 1858–62] became governor-general, and during his tenure, wars with China and Iran took place.

Then came the Mutiny of 1857, leading to the takeover of the Company administration by the British Crown. The event must be remembered for the annexation of the Indian Empire by Her Majesty, Queen Victoria. Her Majesty honoured India by taking it under her blessed protection. A royal proclamation was issued, and its copies were distributed in different vernacular languages throughout the country. The proclamation stated:

> To our loyal subjects in India, we make a solemn promise to you to run the country's affairs with justice and without prejudice, the welfare of the people being uppermost in our mind. You would be trained in any profession, be it artisanship or tradesman-ship. All efforts would be taken to make you people self-reliant and prosperous. This is a matter of firm resolve for us. The prosperity of the subjects in India is a *sine qua non* for the empire. It is a matter of great contentment for us.[15]

Here we believe that our mother's firm promises made by the sovereign queen, have been fully and firmly fulfilled. We observe that the happiness and well-being of the people of India are of prime concern for the British officials in India. Educational institutions of several types are being opened all over. We may be doomed if we do not feel obliged to acknowledge the kindness and patronage of our mother-like queen. Let us pray to the

> Almighty for Her Majesty's long life and pleasure; she is the champion of seven worlds on earth. We also pray for the well-being and happiness of her children, family and all her functionaries.

Hence, with her takeover of the Indian empire, Her Majesty Queen Victoria bestowed upon the governors-general in India the additional honorific of the Viceroy of India. Lord Canning became the first viceroy. After his return in 1862, Lord Elgin [1862–63] took over the position, followed by Lord Lawrence in 1863.[16] A war with Bhutan took place in 1864 and with Abyssinia in 1867. In 1869, Amir Sher Ali Khan of Kabul visited Ambala for a meeting with the viceroy.

In 1869, Lord Mayo [1869–72] became the viceroy. During his time, the Wahabi uprising took place. He went on a visit to Port Blair in the Andamans, where a prisoner named Sher Ali Afridi assassinated him. Lord Northbrook [1872–76] succeeded Lord Mayo as the viceroy in 1872. The high point of his tenure was the great visit of the Prince of Wales to India and the withdrawal of the income tax by Her Majesty.

In 1876, Lord Lytton [1876–80] became the new viceroy, and the historic Dehli *Badādurbār* [grand court] was held on 1 January 1877. It was then that Queen Victoria assumed the title of the Empress of India or *Qaisar e Hind*.[17] In 1879, a licence tax was introduced, the shopping complex adjacent to the Fatehpuri mosque was restored, and the Kabul War began.

Lord Ripon became viceroy in 1887,[18] and the whole of India was beholden to him for many welfare schemes. Meanwhile, he helped Amir Abdur Rahman Khan to take over as the king of Kabul. In 1884, Lord Dufferin [1884–88] became the viceroy of India. His tenure saw the annexation of Burma to the British Empire and the reintroduction of the income tax. Lord Lansdowne took over as viceroy in 1889[19] – a position he occupies to date, and now peace prevails all over the country.

* This was not Warren Hastings, who died in 1818. This Hastings was Francis Edward Rawdon, the 1st Marquess of Hastings, and therefore called Lord Hastings.

Notes

Dehli

1. The author uses spellings Dilli and Dehli for Delhi interchangeably in the text. The chapter is titled Dilli in the original.
2. A *kos* is approximately equal to two miles
3. This is historically inaccurate. More accurate dates are 268–232 BC.
4. The correct spelling is Qutb, but the tower is now known as Qutub Minar.
5. Tarawardi is better known to the students of history as Tarain.
6. Prithviraj Chauhan was captured in what is modern-day Sirsa.

Its medieval name in many accounts is Sarauti, deriving from the mythical Saraswati River, which supposedly once flowed near it.

7. Blake cites Alexander Cunningham, who wrote: '*Qila Marzqhan* (Fort of Refuge), built by Ghiyas ud-Din Balban (1266–87) near the tomb of Nizam ud-Din Auliya, was an asylum for debtors and not a separate citadel or city.' Alexander Cunningham, *Archaeological Survey of India: Four Reports Made During the Years 1862, 63-64-65* (New Delhi: Indological Bookhouse, 1972), I, 133, cited in Stephen P. Blake, *Shahjahanabad, The Sovereign City of Mughal India 1639–1739*, OUP, 1991, 9.
8. Examples of such localities named after the places of their inhabitants' origin include Samarkand, Kashgar, Ghor, and Khata. K.A. Nizami, *Delhi in Historical Perspectives,* trans. Ather Farouqui, OUP, 2020. From here, the author jumps to the reign of Kaiqobad, Balban's grandson. However, Balban himself took over as sultan after Nasiruddin Mahmud. After Balban's son Burgha Khan died in a battle, the reins of the sultanate passed into the hands of Kaiqubad.
9. According to Blake, 'In 1287, soon after his accession, Sultan Kaiqubad began work on a new palace fortress on the banks of the Jamuna [or the Yamuna] at a place called Kailughari.' However, this 'was primarily a place of residence for the emperor, a few nobles, and their servants and retainers; it did not replace Qila Rai Pithora', the capital city established previously by Prithviraj. 'Kaiqubad soon moved back to the old Rajput city.' Y.D. Sharma, *Delhi, and Its Neighbourhood*, 2nd edition (New Delhi: Director

General - Archaeological Survey of India, 1974), 18-19; J. Burton-Page, 'Dehli', in *Encyclopaedia of Islam*, 2nd edition, 256; Mohammad Habib and Khaliq Ahmad Nizami, eds, *The Delhi Sultanat (1206-1526), A Comprehensive History of India*, 5 (Delhi: Peoples' Publishing House, 1970): 304-11, cited in Blake, *Shahjahanabad*: 9–10.

10. This seems to be based on the author's subjective reading of historical facts. Alauddin was arguably the most competent and successful ruler of the Khalji dynasty. He expanded the boundaries of his empire greatly. He also secured the empire's borders against the Mongols, established the rule of law, and ruled for twenty years, during which peace and prosperity prevailed in the country. For more details on the same, see Satish Chandra, *Medieval India: From Sultanat to the Mughals [Part One - Delhi Sultanat [1206–26]*, Delhi, 1997, 75–95.
11. The first ruler of the Tughlaq dynasty.
12. The palace-fortress was named Adilabad or Home of Justice. Blake, *Shahjahanabad*, 10.
13. Leaving Tughlaqabad, 'Muhammad, however, returned to the area around the original Rajput city for the major building project of his reign. Since the Mongols had plundered the heavily built-up area between Qila Rai Pithora and Siri several times, Muhammad ordered a wall to be erected around the suburbs separating the two cities. The enclosure called Jahanpanah (World-Protector) soon became a thriving centre of urban life.' Blake, *Shahjahanabad*, 10.

Nizami tells us that Muhammad Bin also desired 'to encompass Delhi, Siri and Tughlaqabad within a single boundary wall, but his preoccupations with myriad other plans came in the way. Financial constraints, in part, forced him to abandon this grand scheme. He later founded another city, Khurramabad, to commemorate his recognition as king by the Caliph of the day'. Nizami, *Delhi in Historical Perspectives*, 9.

14. The construction of Firozabad is said to have begun in *c.* 1354. According to Shams Siraj Afif, 'The city was spread over an area of ten square miles, and it included Inderpat, Sarai Malik Yar Parran, Sarai Shaikh Abu Bakur Tusi, the mausoleum of Razia Sultan, and Mehrauli. People thronged its busy streets and colourful bazaars. Yet it was easy to move about from place to place because of the availability of various modes of conveyance for hire – *dolis* (palanquins), horses, and bullock carts. A ride in a small cart would cost 4 jetals, and in a bullock cart 6 jetals; a horse could be hired for 12 jetals and a doli for half a tanka.' Shams Siraj Afif, *Tareekh e Feroz Shahi of Shams Siraj Afif*, ed., M. Wilayat Husain (Calcutta: Asiatic Society of Bengal, 1891), 134–36, cited in Nizami, *Delhi in Historical Perspectives*, 10.

    Additionally, 'Kotla Firoze Shah (Palace of Firoze Shah), near the Akbarabadi gate of Shahjahanabad … was the palace-fortress of the emperor.' Sharma, *Delhi and Its Neighbourhood*, 25–26, 129–30; Cunningham, *Archaeological Survey*, I, 218–20, Burton-Page, 'Dehli', 258; Habib and Nizami, *The Delhi Sultanat*, 585–80, cited in Blake, *Shahjahanabad*, 11.

15. The author refers to the Ashokan pillar, which has emperor Ashoka's edicts engraved on it. However, it is unclear why the author calls the pillar sacred for Hindus. Moreover, the pillar was seemingly carted to Firozabad on the boats that floated on the Yamuna. Nizami quotes Afif, who writes, 'Large boats are afloat in the Yamuna, several of them having space for storing 5,000 maunds of foodgrains. Some boats had the capacity for even 7,000 maunds, whereas the smaller boats could store up to 2,000 maunds each.' Afif, *Tareekh e Feroz Shahi of Shams Siraj Afif*, 310, cited in Nizami, *Delhi in Historical Perspectives*, 12.
16. Translated from the original Urdu verse by Insha Allah Khan Insha (1752–1817).
17. Mubarak Shah was succeeded by his nephew Muhammad Shah, and it was during the reign of Aram Shah that the Sayyids lost the throne.
18. The author erroneously gave a Hijri date – 997 AH – which is the equivalent of (or CE) 1589, whereas, by that time, the Mughal empire was firmly established in India under Akbar. Sikandar Lodi died in 1489. Many of the dates given in the book are, in fact, erroneous.
19. The author refers to Alexander III, commonly known as Alexander the Great, the ruler of the ancient Greek kingdom of Macedon from 336 BC to 324 BC, remembered in history as a world conqueror.
20. Bahram refers to a king of Persia, probably Bahram II, who ruled Persia from 274 to 293.

21. A step-well known for its saline water. Now an area in Old Delhi is named after Khari Baoli, and the step-well is lost to time.
22. For various architectural reforms and innovations introduced in the reign of Humayun – including Chahar Taq boats, a floating market, a floating garden, a movable bridge, a movable palace, and a tent of twelve signs – see Khwandamir, *Qanun I Humayuni* or *Humayun Nama*, trans., Baini Prashad (Calcutta: The Baptist Mission Press, 1940): 43–49.
23. Actually, Akbar ascended the throne in 1556.
24. This seems accurate as even Blake, based on his reading of contemporary Mughal accounts, records that 'a massive stone wall 27 feet [9 yards] high, 12 feet [4 yards] thick, and 3.8 miles [approx. 6610 yards] long encircled Shahjahanabad, enclosing an area of about 1500 acres. Erected during 1651–58, this was not the first attempt to enclose the city. A wall of stone and mud had been thrown up in four months during the latter part of 1650 and had promptly collapsed in the monsoon rains of the following year.' Blake, *Shahjahanabad*, 31–32.
25. The author is referring to Zeenat ulMasajid, which has variously been called Ghata Masjid and Ghat Masjid. It exists today.
26. In his account of the daily rituals and the overall way of life of the last two Mughal emperors – Akbar Shah II and Bahadur Shah Zafar – Munshi Faizuddin gives a picturesque description of Hayat Baksh Bagh. He writes, 'The sprawling garden beyond the king's Moti Mahal is known as Hayat Baksh, the dispenser of comfort. Right in the middle is a square-shaped water reservoir

measuring 60 by 60 yards. In the centre of the reservoir stands Jal Mahal, the water palace, flanked on two sides by houses built of white marble. From these houses, the water cascades into the main reservoir. On all four sides, there are four large canals of red stone. Around the canals are flower beds of red brick.' Munshi Faizuddin, *Bazm-i Aakhir*, trans. Ather Farouqui (New Delhi: Roli Books, 2021): 69–70.

27. This is inaccurate. The actual elevation of Delhi is 216 m (709 feet).
28. Translated from the original Persian verse.
29. Translated from the original Persian verse.
30. Surprisingly, the author has missed the names of several Muslim saints of Delhi, including Hazrat Baqi Billah and Hazrat Kalimullah Shah.
31. Here, one is reminded of the fact that the prosperity of the reign of Sultan Alauddin Khalji has often been attributed to the immeasurable blessings of 'the king of Shaikhs, Nizamuddin Aulia'. Additionally, the decline in the fortunes of the sultanate has also been popularly attributed to the removal of such spiritual protection. Alternatively stated, the removal of this spiritual protection has been considered the result of the misconduct of Sultan Firoze Shah Tughlaq, the Shaikhs, the Ulema, and the population of Delhi, as they were unsuccessful in preventing the death of two of Shaikh Sharafuddin Maneri's disciples. When the news of the execution of his disciples reached the Shaikh, he is believed to have said, 'In this city

where they have shed the blood of such holy men – it would be strange if such a city continued to flourish!' Thus, came the downfall of the Sultanate.

In like manner, Sultan Qutbuddin Mubarak is believed to have been hostile towards Shaikh Nizamuddin Aulia. Legend has it that the sultan once summoned the Shaikh on the first of a month and threatened that he would have him brought forcibly. The Shaikh retired to his mother's tomb and submitted the matter to her. The issue was thus taken care of. On the last night before the beginning of the new month, Khusrau Khan, the favourite of the Sultan, treacherously cut off his head, throwing the Sultan's body down from the roof of the palace and setting the head on top of a lance to display it to the populace.

Although it is difficult to extract the hard truth from this morass of embellished stories, the death of Sultan Ghiyasuddin Tughlaq gave rise to one of the best tales of extraordinariness associated with the life of Shaikh Nizamuddin Aulia. Ghiyasuddin is known to have once threatened the Shaikh, probably on his prophecy that the new city of Tughlaqabad built by the sultan would soon be a wilderness. The Sultan was supposed to deal with the Shaikh once he returned from his campaign in the east. While he was on his way back, the Shaikh is said to have pronounced, 'Delhi is yet far away!' (*hunooz Dilli door ast*). Ghiyasuddin was killed by the collapse of a pavilion erected one stage away from the capital. Simon Digby, 'The Sufi Shaykh and the Sultan: A Conflict of Claims to Authority in Medieval India,' *Iran* 28 (1990): 71–74.

A vivid, albeit fictional, account of Ghiyasuddin's discord with Nizamuddin Aulia, through the perspective of a Hindu Kayastha, Musaddi Lal, can also be found in Khushwant Singh's multi-layered novel on the city of Delhi. Khushwant Singh, *Delhi: A Novel* (Delhi: Penguin Random House India, 2016): 81–82.

32. Translated from the original Persian verse.
33. Translated from the original Urdu verse by Mirza Sadiq Sharar (b. circa 1825).
34. This verse is erroneously attributed to the poet Meer Taqi Meer (1723–1810).

A Brief Account of Muslim Monarchs

1. It is surprising to note that an ambitious campaigner like Mahmud Ghaznavi or Ghazni never thought of invading and capturing Delhi, which was popularly acknowledged as the heart of the vast land that was the Indian subcontinent.
2. Shihabuddin Ghori is famous in history as Muhammad Ghori.
3. This seems to be based on the author's subjective reading of historical facts as Prithviraj is, in fact, 'remembered as a great fighter and as a patron of poets and pandits'. Moreover, as a military commander, 'he had many victories to his credit'. Chandra, *Medieval India: [Part One: Delhi Sultanat)]*, 26.

4. In the first chapter, the author uses the place name Tarawadi. This is more accurate, translating into modern-day Tarawadi, situated about 32 km from Thanesar. The battlefield was also spelt as Tarain.
5. Prithviraj's capture, see chapter 1, 'Dehli', note 6.
6. Translated from the original Persian verse.
7. Chandra tells us that '[i]mmediately following the death of Muizzuddin [Shihabuddin/Muhammad Ghori], the Ghurid empire broke up. Muizzuddin's favourite slave, Yalduz, succeeded him at Ghazni, while another enslaved person, Qubacha seized control of Multan and Uchh. Qutbuddin Aibak, who had been deputizing for Muizzuddin at Delhi, was invited by the Turkish armies to Lahore. Aibak marched to Lahore and ascended the throne there … in 1206 based on the support of the local notables and amirs. Although prominent in India, it is doubtful whether he had ever been nominated as his *wali-ahd* (successor or viceroy) by Muizzuddin. Thus, he rose to the throne by personal merit. Somewhat later, he received from Sultan Mahmud, who succeeded his father Ghiyasuddin, at Ghur, a deed of manumission (freeing him from his slave status, legally, an enslaved person could not be a sovereign) and a *chatr*, recognizing his position as a sovereign. This finally ended the legal claim of Ghazni over the Turkish conquests in Hindustan.' Chandra, *Medieval India: [Part One: Delhi Sultanat]*, 37–38.
8. This chapter is followed by a table containing a list of the 'Muslim monarchs' who ruled over India. They belong to the Slave dynasty,

the Khalji dynasty, the Tughlaq dynasty, the Sayyid dynasty, the Lodi dynasty and the Mughal dynasty. Interestingly, the author's list of Mughal monarchs begins with Shah Jahan. As he writes under the column titled 'Remarks', the reason is that before Shah Jahan's rule, Agra was the Mughal capital rather than Delhi.

Story of the Muslim Rule in India from 588 AH [1192] to 1273 AH [1759]

1. The author often uses Ghor and Ghazni interchangeably. The Ghorid and the Ghaznavid dynasties were two distinct dynasties ruling in Afghanistan, although at different times, one captured the other's territories.
2. This is historically inaccurate. As has already been mentioned, Shihabuddin Muhammad Ghori made only two attempts, in the second of which he succeeded in capturing Delhi and Ajmer.
3. Qutbuddin Aibak was the son-in-law of Yalduz, another of Muhammad Ghori's slaves. After Ghori's death, Aibak had to fight Yalduz to control Ghurid territories in north-western India. Yalduz succeeded Ghori at Ghazni.
4. The author uses the name Ghorid for what was the Mamluk (slave) dynasty founded by Muhammad Ghori's slave Qutbuddin Aibak.
5. It lasted 331 years, from 1526 to 1857, and there were nineteen rulers of the dynasty, starting with Babur and ending with Bahadur Shah Zafar.

6. The eighth month of the Islamic calendar.
7. The author ascribes the title of *Tutī-yi Hind* to Muhammad Ibrahim Zauq, the poet laureate of the Mughal court till 1854 – the year of his passing away. However, poet Amir Khusrau (1253–1325) is often referred to as *Tutī-yi Hind* (parrot of India/ voice of India). The title of Zauq was *Khaqani-e Hind* (the poet Khaqani of India).
8. Translated from the original Urdu verse.

The Decline and Ruin of the City of Dehli

1. The author uses Dilli and Dehli interchangeably in the text. The chapter here is titled Dehli, the version in the original.
2. Translated from the original Urdu verse.
3. This struggle for succession resulted in Bahadur Shah I (r. 1707–12) taking over the reins of the empire.
4. As Zahiruddin Malik tells us, there existed such dissatisfaction with the existing state of affairs that it began to show in terms of 'secret consultations and conspiracies among the nobles opposed to the Saiyids'. Significantly, '[t]he elements of the opposition centred around Qudsia Begum', Muhammad Shah's mother. 'She was a shrewd lady, who also possessed a talent of no mean order for undercover intrigue'. Thus, '[a]nxious to emancipate her son, she quickly discovered the instrument she could employ for the purpose. She set to work with Muhammad Amin Khan, the influential leader of the Turani faction and an adept in the art of

intrigue and dissimulation, to prepare schemes for the overthrow of the Saiyids'. Zahiruddin Malik, *The Reign of Muhammad Shah 1719–1748* (New Delhi: Asia Publishing House, 1977), 58–59.

5. This is again based on the author's subjective interpretation of historical facts. As pointed out by Malik, Muhammad Shah 'has long been misjudged' and is often painted 'as a debauch, indolent and careless king'. He is also considered 'exclusively responsible for the decay and ruin of the Empire'. However, it was, in fact, a fatal combination of circumstances rather than the weakness of the man at the helm, which was responsible for the ultimate collapse of the empire. Malik, *The Reign of Muhammad Shah*, viii.
6. Here, it needs to be added that Nadir Shah, an ambitious non-Iranian, because of his military prowess, had captured Iran's (Persia's) throne and had expanded his empire far and wide to the Arab lands. He had no apparent intention of capturing or ruling the Indian subcontinent. He simply had his eyes on the subcontinent's unmatched wealth, including the world-famous Peacock Throne and the priceless Kohinoor diamond. But to achieve this, he unleashed a holocaust in the city of Delhi.
7. After he had fled from Delhi in fear of his life from his father's (Alamgir II's) all-powerful wazir Imadul Mulk (Ghaziuddin Khan Feroz Jung III).
8. An accepted narrative leading to this event is that Ghulam Qadir's father, Zabita Khan, had allied with the Sikhs against the Mughal rule but was defeated in 1777. Zabita Khan fled, but his

son was captured. Later, teenage Ghulam Qadir was castrated (and made a harem eunuch) on the pretext of his conspiring to assassinate Emperor Shah Alam but probably as a punishment for his father's rebellion. Ghulam Qadir, in turn, occupied Delhi in 1788 and took revenge by blinding the emperor and sacking the fort.

9. Mahadeoji Scindia was an old ally of Shah Alam II and was asked to become the empire's regent.
10. The son and successor of Ahmed Shah Durrani.
11. The pen name under which the emperor wrote.
12. Synoptically translated into English from the Urdu translation of the Persian poem chronicled by the author.
13. While the author records the year to be 1802, it was actually in 1803 that General Lake defeated Daulat Scindia, Mahadeoji Scindia's successor, and captured the city of Delhi.
14. Translated from the original Urdu verse by Mirza Saeeduddin Ahmad Khan Talib Dehlavi (1852–1919).
15. The second month of the Islamic calendar.
16. This is the English translation of the Urdu version of the document recorded in the text.
17. Richard Wellesley was the governor-general from 1798 to 1805 and Sir George Hilaro Barlow from 1805 to 1807. This is the English translation of the Urdu version of the document recorded in the text.
18. With the introduction of new Enfield rifles in the British Indian Army, rumours spread that their cartridges, whose covers had

to be torn open with the mouth, were greased with pig and cow fat, and so offending the religious sentiments of both Hindu and Muslim soldiers. It was these rumours that acted as the immediate trigger for the Revolt of 1857.

19. Prince Mirza Muhammad Hidayat Afza alias Mirza Ilahi Baksh was a close confidant of Bahadur Shah and father-in-law to his son Mirza Fatehul Mulk alias Mirza Fakhru. In reality, what has been presented as an act of extreme kindness by the English was a reward for Ilahi Baksh's role in aiding the English in the smooth arrest of the emperor in the aftermath of the revolt. Ilahi Baksh was, in fact, a member of Hodson's spy network and thus instrumental in the arrest of Bahadur Shah Zafar by the English at Humayun's Tomb. 'For his services, he was given the title of *Shehzada* and chief representative and head of the Royal House of Timur. The British also gave him an annual pension of Rs 22,830. He lived in Rang Mahal in Suiwalan.' Munshi Faizuddin, *Bazm-i Aakhir*, xv. He was also known as the Traitor of Delhi.
20. The author does not mention the official designations of either James Loyal or R. Clark. The translator has been unable to fill this gap.

An Account of Existing Monuments in Shahjahanabad, Dehli

1. This is in accurate. Roshan Ara was the daughter of Shah Jahan and was, in fact, Aurangzeb's sister. In his revolt against his father,

she sided with Aurangzeb.

2. But the date given in the dates column is 1178 AH, in the Delhi Urdu Academy Edition. This page is missing in the 1894 edition.
3. Yet the compiler has included it in the list of existing monuments.
4. There is a discrepancy of dates here between the year of construction column and the date Jalaluddin Khilji came to the throne. There are several such discrepancies in the dates in the table. While the table has been compiled by Maghrub Abidi, the notes are by the translator.
5. Sabz Burj was built in 1530 and predates Humayun's tomb

The British at the Helm of India

1. This is inaccurate as Thomas Roe arrived in India in 1615 in the court of Jahangir.
2. The author is referring to Queen Elizabeth I. The hijri date given here by the author is clearly wrong since its equivalent is 1800, off by almost two centuries!
3. An unclear anecdote following this has been omitted in the translation.
4. Here, the original text is somewhat unclear. Hence, a few words have been omitted since they do not significantly impact the continuity of the author's argument.
5. This includes the Battle of Plassey of 1757.
6. Warren Hastings became the governor-general in 1773 and held the position till 1785.

7. The author is referring to the Second Anglo-Mysore War (1780–84), a conflict between the kingdom of Mysore and the British East India Company.
8. Lord Cornwallis succeeded Warren Hastings as governor-general in 1786.
9. As the third of the four Anglo-Mysore wars, this occurred between 1790 and 1792. The conflict involved the kingdom of Mysore, the East India Company, Travancore, the Maratha Empire and the Nizam of Hyderabad.
10. Sir George Barlow's term of office as governor-general was from 1805 to 1807.
11. Lord Minto occupied the post of the governor-general from 1807 to 1813.
12. The Treaty of Amritsar with Mahraja Ranjit Singh was signed in 1809.
13. The First Burmese War took place between 1824 and 1826.
14. The author skips Lord Hardinge's tenure from 1844 to 1848 and moves on to Lord Dalhousie.
15. This is the English translation of the Urdu document recorded in the book.
16. Lord John Lawrence's term of office as Viceroy of India was from 1864 to 1869.
17. Although Queen Victoria did not attend the *durbar* in person.
18. This is probably a typographical error, as following this, the author mentions Lord Dufferin's term of office beginning in 1884. Additionally, this is historically inaccurate as Lord Ripon

became the viceroy of India in 1880 and continued in office till 1884.

19. Either a typographical error or a historical inaccuracy as Lord Lansdowne served as the viceroy from 1888 to 1894.